MOSCOW

WOMEN

MOSCOW

THIRTEEN INTERVIEWS BY

CAROLA HANSSON AND KARIN LIDÉN

Translated by Gerry Bothmer, George Blecher, and Lone Blecher

INTRODUCTION BY GAIL WARSHOFSKY LAPIDUS

PANTHEON BOOKS NEW YORK

WOMEN

Library of Congress Cataloging in Publication Data
Samtal med kvinnor i Moskva. English.
Moscow women.
Translation of: Samtal med kvinnor i Moskva.
Bibliography: p.
1. Women—Russian S. F. S. R.—Moscow—Case studies.
I. Hansson, Carola.
II. Lidén, Karin, 1941–
III. Title.
HQ1665.M6S2513 1983   305.4'0947'312   82-18841
ISBN 0-394-52332-6
ISBN 0-394-71491-1 (paperback)
Manufactured in the United States of America
98765432
Book Design: Elissa Ichiyasu

CONTENTS

INTRODUCTION

This collection of interviews with thirteen Moscow women is a unique document. While it forms an integral part of a growing body of studies of women's roles in the Soviet Union and other socialist systems, it is the first to offer a glimpse into the lives of Soviet women as experienced by the women themselves. It conveys, in their own words, the hopes and disappointments, the trials and small triumphs, and above all the grinding daily burdens of everyday existence as they seek to strike some balance between work and family roles. It adds both a distinctive and a complementary perspective to the portrait of Soviet women's lives offered by Western scholarly treatments, by Soviet fiction, and by the underground writings of Soviet feminists, now available in translation.

How these interviews came about and how the tapes eventually reached Stockholm is a story in itself. What would be a relatively simple journalistic undertaking in the West was fraught with difficulties and dangers in Moscow. The very existence of this volume is therefore a tribute to the ingenuity of its authors as well as to the courage and frankness of the Soviet women who participated in the effort.

The themes that are central to this work can best be understood in the broader context of Soviet development and the particular role that women have occupied in it. As in Western Europe and the United States, the "woman question" in Russia had its origins in the nineteenth century, when advocates of political and social reform incorporated a commitment to sexual equality into their broader programs of emancipation. The Bolshevik revolution of 1917 proclaimed the full liberation of women and granted them equal political and civil rights, but the central thrust of the Marxist-Leninist perspective emphasized female employment as the condition of full equality, not only in the wider society but within the family itself. By the Stalin period, however, the very image of women's liberation had been transformed. Where the revolutionary theorists viewed employment as a way of enhancing women's status and independence and sought to free women from family responsibilities by shifting these to the socialized sector, the economic and social transformations of the Stalin period simply added industrial employment to women's traditional family roles. The Five-Year Plans, which created enormous demands for workers, combined with the social and demographic effects of World War I, civil war, collectivization, purges, and then of World War II, transformed wives and widows into heads of households and deprived a large proportion of Soviet women of the opportunity to marry. The shortage of men not only increased the pressure upon women to enter the labor force; it also had its impact on culture and psychology. On the one hand, it strengthened a long tradition of the "strong woman" in Russian culture by placing a great premium on the qualities of toughness and independence, requisites of sheer survival during these years. On the other hand, it enhanced the value of —and nostalgia for—a more traditional feminine role in which family-oriented values occupied a central place.

By the end of World War II women constituted over half the Soviet labor force, and in the face of the continuing labor shortage of the postwar years, female participation rates outside agriculture continued to rise. Today, virtually all women outside Central Asia and the Caucasus are either employed or studying, almost all full-time. While work is clearly a source of both status and genuine personal satisfaction, these interviews testify to the role that financial pressures play as well. Two incomes are essential to support a family above what even Soviet economists would consider the poverty level. Moreover, because the possibility and desirability of part-time employment are only now being debated in the Soviet Union, women with young children are forced to choose between the exhaustion of full-time work and the isolation and limited horizons of remaining at home.

At the same time, the burden of household responsibilities is far greater in the Soviet Union than in other countries at comparable levels of development. Because Stalin's economic policies attached such high priority to the development of heavy industry and the military sector, the consumer sector and the services needed to supply it were deliberately sacrificed. An underdeveloped system of retail trade, combined with severe shortages and irregularities in the supply of consumer goods and services, makes shopping in the Soviet Union an extraordinarily time-consuming activity. It is a kind of "hunting and gathering" operation that requires locating supplies of desired goods, waiting in long queues in a multiplicity of small stores or departments to obtain them, and carrying heavy parcels over long distances by train and bus at the end of a long workday to get them home.

Housing was another victim of Stalinist priorities, as well as of the devastation wrought by World War II. Despite the large investments in new apartment construction that Khrushchev initiated, Soviet urban families continue to live in cramped apartments lacking in basic amenities. Almost a quarter of them still occupy communal apartments where kitchen and bath are shared with other occupants; young families often crowd into a single room in dormitory accommodations provided by enterprises or educational institutions. New projects with individual apartments have long waiting lists, unless a family has sufficient capital to purchase a cooperative apartment of its own. Typically, it is young couples and newlyweds who face the hardest time finding living space and a modicum of privacy; these interviews offer eloquent testimony to their preoccupation with housing, and to the importance of the informal but often complex exchanges that contribute to even limited solutions.

During the Stalin period, it was only in the area of child care, so essential to massive female labor-force participation, that economic priorities and revolutionary commitments meshed. The Soviet commitment to extensive public child-care facilities derived from three distinct objectives: to permit the employment of mothers, to provide an environment more suitable than that of the family for the proper socialist upbringing of children, and to capitalize on the economies of scale. The system of public child care that gradually developed was composed of three types of institutions that together embraced about one-third of Soviet preschoolers by 1982: crèches or nurseries for infants and children under the age of three, kindergartens for the group aged three to seven, and combined nursery-kindergartens introduced in 1959 to provide a more unified learning experience. Despite the enormous expansion of this network in recent years and its central role in the daily lives of working mothers, it suffers from a number of problems widely discussed in the Soviet press and further illuminated by these interviews. First, the availability of places, particularly at the better-quality institutions, falls short of the demand. The quality of the centers varies widely, and the staffing is a particular subject of complaints. The ratio of children to staff is extremely high and the quality and training of personnel relatively low, since the profession is ranked rather low in both status and income. The exposure of children to disease is a perennial problem, compounded by the absence of special provisions for the care of sick children. The high rate of illness and absenteeism in turn disrupts the work schedules of mothers. Finally, child-care centers are often located at considerable distances from the parents' places of employment, necessitating long and arduous trips by public transportation before and after working hours. In the case of single mothers such as Liza, whose interview opens the book, the burden may prove so great that the child is placed in a boarding facility and returns home only for weekends. All in all, Soviet families are less than enthusiastic about such institutional care, particularly for very young children, and it is often the absence of alternatives rather than a positive preference that dictates their use. New mothers generally choose to remain at home for the first year of a child's life, aided by provisions for maternity leave with partial pay. If a grandmother or other close female relative is available, the child may then be left in her care to permit the young mother to return to work.

With this background in mind, it is clear that the balancing of work and family roles is a central problem in the lives of Soviet women. For several decades, official Soviet writings ignored the problem, insisting that the Soviet Union was the first society in history to have achieved sexual equality and that if no feminist movement existed in the USSR, it was because the "woman question" had been finally solved. By the mid-1960s, however, the question of women's roles had emerged once again as a subject of serious public discussion. The starting point of such discussions was the recognition that the dual roles of women create contradictions that even a socialist society cannot easily resolve. As ritual self-congratulation began to give way to serious discussion of "shortcomings" and "contradictions" in Soviet everyday life, a growing array of scholarly studies by economists, sociologists, and demographers—many of them women—began to document in some detail a long list of problems: low levels of skill, income, and mobility among women workers; the heavy and conflicting demands of their dual roles; the harmful effects of poor working conditions and inadequate social services on their health and well-being and that of their families. Rising divorce rates and declining birthrates provoked particular concern, challenging as they did the comfortable assumption that under socialism economic progress and social stability went hand in hand. Trade-union conferences and party meetings as well as scholarly symposia began to devote themselves to discussions of female work and family roles, and Brezhnev himself acknowledged, in a 1977 speech, that "we . . . men have thus far done far from all we could to ease the dual burden that [women] bear both at home and in production."

Official public discussion formed only the tip of a far larger iceberg of private dissatisfaction. Natalya Baranskaya's evocation of "a week like any other" in the harried life of a young scientific worker, wife, and mother gave fictional expression to the stresses and conflicts faced by millions of her counterparts in daily life. Two decades later the samizdat publication of the first Soviet feminist journal, with its implicit repudiation of the official view that the "woman question" had been solved in the Soviet Union, would result in the expulsion from the USSR of its four founding editors, a dramatic revelation of official sensitivities.

But this feminist effort expressed an activism only rarely encountered among Soviet women. Far more typical are the attitudes of resignation and even fatalism expressed in these thirteen interviews. On the one hand, everyday experience points to the unequal position that women in fact occupy: the extra burden of family as well as work roles; the low salaries and status that go with occupations clearly recognized as "women's work"; the limited participation of men in domestic responsibilities. There is a clear recognition that men have choices which women do not; as Lyalya admits, she cannot think of anything that makes women's lives better than men's. What is equally poignant is the acceptance of the view that this is indeed equality. As Liza puts it, "Our women suffer from equality"; or, in the words of Anna, "With emancipation, we lead such abnormal, twisted lives because women have to work the same as men do." Trapped by an official ideology that defines equality in a particular way, and unable to challenge that definition, they perceive their situation as inevitable, unchangeable. The gap between experience and consciousness is never bridged.

The potential impact of Western feminist values and perspectives on the consciousness of Soviet women is limited by several factors. First, as these interviews make abundantly clear, Soviet women have a very incomplete and distorted image of the feminist program, one shaped largely by its treatment in Soviet media. To the extent that it involves demands long since enshrined in Soviet law, such as legalized abortion or equal rights, the movement appears irrelevant to Soviet conditions. To the extent that Western feminism is perceived as embodying attitudes of hostility toward men or a critical view of the family as a social institution, it holds little attraction for the average Soviet woman. On the other hand, there is little knowledge or appreciation of the fundamental concerns of Western feminism, and in particular of its commitment to more flexible sex roles, to personal fulfillment, and to enhanced freedom of choice of social roles for women, concerns that would strike a responsive chord in Soviet women.

A number of the themes running through these interviews have a distinctively Russian character. Primary among them is the enormous value attached to children. They are described as a major goal in life, the main satisfaction, and the preoccupation that most distinguishes women from men. It is also clear that these mothers pay an extremely high price for having and raising children, both materially and psychologically. The insufficiency of time and energy for their proper care is a constant refrain, and an undercurrent of guilt runs through many of these accounts. As a consequence, several of these Moscow women talk of a gap between the number of children they would ideally like to have and the one or two that seem in fact possible, a gap that has shown up in large-scale Soviet opinion surveys as well. Indeed, many of the current policy debates center on the question why Soviet urban families in the European regions of the country are having so few children, thus contributing to an unwelcome slowdown in population growth, and what policy measures might reverse this alarming trend.

Sexual issues are a somewhat awkward topic of discussion, and the interviews convey a lack of basic knowledge about the whole question. Several women express their embarrassment in talking about intimate matters, but mention the lack of any formal sex education, their ignorance about the subject well into adulthood, and the fact that in several cases their first child was unintended. The interviews also reveal many misconceptions about contraceptive methods, a high reliance on a combination of home remedies and taking chances, and an ultimate dependence on abortion as a major method of birth control, however traumatic the entire experience proves to be. These interviews tend to support the information from other sources that contraceptives are of poor quality and in limited use in the Soviet Union, that men are unwilling to use condoms and women perceive the pill to be dangerous, that anxiety about possible pregnancy is extremely high, and that urban women have exceedingly large numbers of abortions as a consequence.

The importance of family ties is another striking theme in this book. Many of these women express an extraordinary degree of closeness to their parents, consider them a central influence on their values and tastes, and remain highly dependent on their families of origin, both psychologically and materially, well into adulthood. Families support them as students and young adults, affording the margin of economic assistance that lifts them above subsistence level. They furnish such major capital gifts as apartments, refrigerators, other durables, and winter coats, and they are especially important in helping with housing arrangements and exchanges to provide living space for young couples. Their services are equally essential, whether in delivering a home-cooked meal to a harried young mother or providing the only baby-sitting services available given the absence of such a profession in the Soviet Union. Finally, they offer enormous emotional and psychological support to their offspring, especially critical when young marriages break up and single mothers are left to care for children alone, an increasingly common phenomenon in the Soviet Union as divorce rates reach American levels.

Finally, there is the idealized image of femininity with which these conversations are suffused. Women are portrayed as the bearers of values, of morality, culture, history, religion, honesty, and conscience; they are burdened with the responsibilities of perfection itself, and the women berate themselves for their constant inability to live up to this ideal. The image of men is similarly romanticized and the reality is similarly disappointing: the women yearn for men who are strong, protective, and good fathers, and find instead men who drink heavily, refuse to share housework, and have limited interest in children. The tension between the value attached to independence and the chasm of unfulfilled dependent needs is enormous.

Underlying all the other themes is the gap between desires and possibilities. Whether the desire is for a higher standard of living and beautiful clothes, or for more free time and the leisure to read and write and care for children, or for greater opportunities for travel and entertainment, or simply for an easier life, the interviews convey an unfulfilled yearning for the opportunity to express individuality and little confidence that this yearning can be satisfied.

Gail Warshofsky Lapidus
ASSOCIATE PROFESSOR OF POLITICAL SCIENCE,
UNIVERSITY OF CALIFORNIA AT BERKELEY

PREFACE

In the spring of 1978 we interviewed a number of women in Moscow, all of whom we had met through personal rather than official contacts. Our interviews were tape-recorded; thirteen of them are included in this book.

From what we had read, and also from what we had observed during our many earlier visits, we felt that the emancipation of women in the Soviet Union had come to a halt in midcourse. We knew that Soviet women work outside the home, perhaps more than women in any other country. We also realized that despite the official talk about equality, the responsibility for children and the household is still placed squarely on women, and that this is used as an excuse to discriminate against them in the work force.

We had seen the problems they contend with, including bad housing conditions; long, tiring commutes between home and work; food shortages; and endless lines for supplies. We had met and become friends with many women, and we had been filled with admiration for the strength and self-confidence they radiated despite the many hardships of their lives.

We sought to discover in these interviews how the women themselves regarded their life-style. Were they aware of the implications of their situation? Did they discuss them? What did they consider their greatest problems? Did they envision any solutions? Did they feel imprisoned by the ingrained sex roles that characterize Soviet society? How were they able to manage their double roles as workers and as wives and mothers?

We are reluctant to say much about how we obtained the interviews for fear of harming the women who so generously spoke with us, but a few words are in order. Needless to say, we could not simply enter the country with tape recorders in hand. We made a short preliminary trip to Moscow to see whether we'd be able to borrow the necessary equipment when the time came, and we made arrangements with a number of women to interview them when we came back.

We then returned for a longer period, borrowed a tape recorder, and contacted the women we planned to interview. Some never turned up; others we managed to meet. We interviewed them in their homes, in Russian, without an interpreter. We had tourist visas, and no authorities were involved. The women were all enormously eager to speak, interested in our questions, and very outspoken.

We were forced to leave the tapes in Moscow at the end of the trip, and more than six months passed before we received them in Stockholm through private channels. They were faithfully transcribed for the book, but the names used are not the women's real names, nor are they pictured in the photos.

Of course, it is difficult to give a complete picture of the situation of Soviet women in thirteen interviews. Yet a number of important patterns did emerge, and these are discussed in greater length in the short chapters between the interviews and in the postscript.

We are indebted to the women whose voices are heard here; without their frankness and generosity, we could never have written this book.

Carola Hansson
Stockholm

Karin Lidén
Paris

1982

M O S C O W

W O M E N

L I Z A

"IT'S TERRIFYING WHEN A WOMAN SPEAKS.
THE TRUTH COMES OUT AND THE REAL PAIN EMERGES."

*L**iza is twenty-eight years old and works as an editor in a
publishing house. We meet her first in her brother's home. She
is wearing a long red robe with a deep décolletage, has blond
curly hair, wears black mascara. Her eyelids are pale blue and
her lips a dark rose.*

*She doesn't walk into the room; she makes an entrance. She sits
down across from us, gives us an inquisitive, amused look, and immediately opens the conversation by asking us about our lives.*

*The night we intend to interview her she opens the door with an
exclamation of pleasure. She seems delighted to see us and to play the
role of hostess. This time she is wearing a long, tight, ruffled dress
with a turn-of-the-century look and platform sandals. She invites us
to sit down in her kitchen, one of the most impractically arranged we
have ever seen. The stove is in one corner, the small sink in the other,
and in the middle, with hardly any space to move around, is a small
table. A few watercolors depicting beautiful Russian summer land-
scapes are tacked up on the walls, a reminder of what exists outside
this bleak high-rise kitchen.*

Liza immediately serves us wine, and she and a friend scurry around preparing dinner: meat and a salad. She says that this is the first time she is cooking meat, that she is impractical and hates to cook. From time to time she pours water into the frying pan, takes a sip of wine, looks around for forks. She wants us to tell her about life in the West, tries to persuade her friend to sing Russian folk songs, and then suddenly sits down at the table and with utmost seriousness and deep concentration begins to recite some of her own poems.

When we interview her she is deeply absorbed in her thoughts, her moods constantly changing. One moment she talks with a gleam in her eye and ironic distance, laughing and gesticulating enthusiastically; the next moment she becomes serious and quiet. At times she is upset and indignant, and then suddenly she has tears in her eyes.

Tell us something about yourself.

I'm twenty-eight. I have a degree in literature and work for a publishing house. I have a son, Emil. I had a husband, who was an artist, but now he's gone. We got married in 1970 and divorced in 1975, I think.

I own my apartment, which my father bought for me, since it's so difficult to get an apartment here; for someone my age it's totally impossible. I lived here with my husband, and now I live here alone.

What is your daily routine like? Can you tell us what you did yesterday, for instance?

I got up at seven o'clock and went to work. Mostly I have to travel during rush hours; the streetcar was so crowded that I was almost knocked down . . . horrible.

Oh no! Yesterday was Monday! I woke at six, pulled my child out of bed, packed a bag full of stuff for the whole week, and then he and I took off for the subway. The *two* of us were practically knocked down. A woman was sitting and reading

4

and wouldn't give up her seat, even though my son was squashed against the doors. He almost fell on her, and I tightened my grip to keep him from falling and getting hurt. I told him, "Emil, a child could die in front of that woman while she sat there reading. Don't you ever be like that." It took us fifty minutes to get to the day-care center.

I took him inside and undressed him and then I had to rush off to work. He cried, "Mama, I don't want to stay here. I want to go home." I said, "Emil, sweetheart, please stay in the day-care center now. I'll come and get you soon. I'll pick you up on Friday." And yesterday was Monday. It was terrible, but I had to hurry off to work.

I left him crying. The teachers took him by the arm and brought him over to the group because I couldn't stay to comfort him. I picked up my things and put my shawl over my head. Outside it was still rush hour. And I was going to the opposite end of Moscow. It was another hour's trip, and I was already late for work. When I dashed out of the subway I was planning to transfer to a bus, and I felt as if I were about to have a minor heart attack. But the bus was just pulling away, so I had to run instead, knowing I'd be in trouble because I was late. I was trying to work out a scheme. If only there were an open window at my office so that I could throw my stuff in and crawl in after it! That way no one would know I was late.

However, the windows were closed, and I quickly ran in. There was a lot of work on my desk. First on the agenda was a weekly report. There was also a lot of mail, proofreading and editing. Then I had to race around to various departments, pick up files, etc. After lunch I became terribly drowsy because I had hardly slept all night long. I was absentminded and couldn't seem to pull myself together. Later when I felt I couldn't stand it any longer we sent someone for a bottle of wine. Sometimes we do that where I work. Yesterday, toward the end of the day, we drank a big glass of port to clear our heads.

Then, exhausted, I dropped by my parents' since I hadn't prepared any food at home. I knew they would have something for me. Afterwards I watched television—one of those series. I was too tired to think or read, although I had a book that had been hard to get my hands on. It had been such a difficult day. So that's what my day was like yesterday, a typical Monday.

So Emil's at the day-care center all week. Is he there at night as well?

Yes, it's called weekly boarding school. I could pick him up on Wednesdays, but it doesn't seem to work out. If I fetch him after work we don't get home until eight. He goes to bed at nine, and then I have to get up at six to get him back to the day-care center. The rush again, the mobs. That isn't good for him. He might catch influenza since he wears his little fur coat in the subway, although it's terribly hot and he's soaked with perspiration when we get into the street to walk to the center. As a result he has a cold almost the whole winter.

Does he like the boarding school?

It's O.K. By Friday when I pick him up he's happy. He's been playing with his friends and it's hard to tear him away. He's gotten used to it. But on Monday it's the same story all over again.

Doesn't his father spend time with him?

No, he rarely sees his father. The situation is complicated. When the baby was born I gave him my surname. I decided that since I had had to carry the whole burden and I suffered the most, I wanted to give him my name. His father was very upset that the boy didn't have his name. They almost never see each other, although Emil is the image of his father. He never gets anything from him, but I do get alimony, 35 rubles a month.*

* One ruble (divided into 100 kopeks) is currently equivalent to around $1.36.

How do you spend your free time?

Saturdays and Sundays are mostly devoted to my child. When he sleeps I have some time to read, but a lot of my energy goes into him. Free time? Yes, on weekdays after work. Of course I'm tired, but at least I can do as I please. Sometimes when I have a few moments I try to write; I couldn't imagine not writing. I'll probably write all my life—how regularly I don't know, since I don't have the time. But when I have a free evening I write poetry.

How much time do you spend on your household? Shopping, for instance.

I have an easier time than most because of my parents. When I can't bear to do the shopping—because as sure as anything I'll start arguing with someone, complain to the manager, or hit somebody; that's just the way I am—and when I can't stand the mass of people, the crowd, the confusion, and I need to be alone, I go to my parents' and my mother feeds me.

My relationship with my parents is very good. Of course we argue, but we argue with an understanding of each other, because I'm like them in my way of thinking. We always enjoy each other's company. I share my most intimate thoughts with them—especially with my father. When we talk I don't feel that he's older than I am—we're the same age in our souls.

When I was a child that feeling was even stronger—one of us could tell what the other was thinking, even if we were apart. It's said that Blok* had a similar relationship with his mother; for me it's with my father.

I remember that when I was about five, he was going through a difficult time. I was in a country day-care center; I was restless and couldn't sleep—I sensed that Papa was having a hard time. Then we went to Moscow and I asked him why. Something had happened. I remember the incident so clearly.

* Alexander Blok (1880–1921) was a Russian Symbolist poet.

7

A poet—he's dead now—had written an article criticizing him. I didn't understand any of this, since I couldn't read, but I sensed that Papa was in trouble. We had always been able to communicate—even better before I was married. Then we used to travel together. He is a poet and often makes public appearances. I appeared on the stage with him and read his poems.

In this country when children leave their family they seldom think about their parents; children and parents usually don't understand each other. The children take off when they're about seventeen and get married. When children and parents have to live together they live as neighbors in a joint or communal apartment.* But the children have to obey their parents. There's a saying in our country: If you spit on old people you spit on your country; if you spit on your ancestors you spit in your own face.

Were you born in Moscow?

Yes. Six of us lived in a room twenty square meters in size, which was part of a communal apartment. It was Mama's room. Papa wasn't born in Moscow; he came from . . . the frontier you could say, from the country. He married my mother and settled down in that room. There was also Mama's sister, Grandmother, and I, and then my brother, Alyosha, was born. As a young girl Mama had lived in a whole apartment. Then in 1937 her father was put in prison. If my grandmother had divorced him she could have avoided going with him and could have stayed with her three children. But she didn't think it was right to divorce him after he was jailed, so she went to prison for eight years as a family member of an enemy of the people. When the children were left alone they were forced to leave their apartment, which consisted only of two rooms— small ones at that—even though her husband had had an im-

* Because of the continued shortage of housing in Moscow and other large cities, it is still common for several families to share an apartment with a communal kitchen and bathroom but separate living/sleeping quarters.

portant position in the government. They were kicked out, and my mother, who was sixteen at the time, was left with two small children. Her youngest sister was three, and the authorities wanted to put her in an orphanage, but the family pleaded with them, and finally she was allowed to stay. She had a very interesting life, my aunt, but you came to talk about me. . . .

How do you remember your childhood?

I think I had a very happy childhood, so happy that . . . Marina Tsvetayeva* writes that her childhood was so happy that when she reached sixteen she wanted to die. We did live under difficult circumstances. Papa used to block himself off in a corner to write, which gave the room a cramped look; he wrote some of his most important works right there in that corner. The neighbors were impossible; they were always playing the violin and the double bass. It was a terrible life, and still Papa kept on writing. . . . We had nothing. Now we have a summer cottage and everything, but at that time nothing.

When I was born they had only potatoes on the table to celebrate my birth. They didn't have the money for a baby carriage, so they put me in a basket which Papa hung outside the window. We lived on the second floor, and the boys would throw stones at the basket—they thought it was fruit or something. On the whole, I remember my childhood as very happy —especially my relationship with my father. I just remember specific incidents, episodes. . . . He wasn't a believer, but I get tears in my eyes when I remember how he used to take me to church. It was in an old cloister, and I still go back sometimes —my deepest roots are there. He introduced me to music and literature—everything I learned was through him. As I grew up, the stories he used to tell me still came to mind, but as I discovered what life was like, they began to collapse like a house of cards. There was a period in my life—I think I was in

* Russian poet (1892–1941).

eighth grade—when I wanted to commit suicide. I thought life was horrible compared to the images I had from childhood. But my father did manage to give me a kind of inner strength. He came from peasant stock, and he probably gave me a peasant approach to life. Peasants rarely commit suicide, because no matter what happens, starvation or whatever, their ties to the soil restrain them.

School was terrible—a nightmare. In our schools the individual is put down as much as possible. If a child tries to express original thoughts—if he sets himself apart from the group—he's reprimanded and reduced to the same level as the others. I think about writing a story about my school in which only those children who got D's would turn out to be talented people. In our school we competed in how to please the teacher and in memorizing our lessons. Of course there were good teachers. I remember a very good literature teacher. I liked her and she liked me. We understood each other.

When I was in either seventh or eighth grade my classmates drank and lived a wild life, although they were all members of Komsomol.* At that time I wanted to work with problem children. We have many such specialized schools.

What were your main interests in your early teens?

At fifteen I already loved Dostoevsky, and my ideal was Prince Myshkin.† I fell in love with a boy who I thought was like him, although he wasn't at all. I loved classical music—I couldn't stand jazz, but now I love it—but once, while I was listening to my kind of music, sitting in a dark room, he pointed to me and said to his pals, "She's crazy!" He loved the Beatles, who were very popular then. End of the affair.

I fell in love easily—at the day-care center and with the boys in elementary school.

---

* The Soviet Communist Party's youth organization. Members are between fifteen and twenty-eight years old. Almost all young people belong to the organization.
† The protagonist of Dostoevsky's *The Idiot.*

I also had a girl friend I was very fond of. My parents forbade me to associate with her since she came from a so-called "undesirable" family. When her father was on business trips her mother brought lovers to the house. But she remained my friend, and as an excuse I told my parents that I wanted to help "pull her out of the mud."

One day at school I got bawled out by a teacher, and my friend said, "Please move me. I don't want to sit next to her." That was almost the end of our friendship. Later we lost contact with each other—we came from entirely different worlds. She was from a working-class family, and she never went beyond the eighth grade. I wrote a story about her. She worked in a factory and had a lot of unfortunate affairs, following completely in her mother's footsteps. When I invited her to my home she drank all the vodka she was given, but when I wanted to read a poem she said, "No, you know I don't understand that poetry stuff."

I had another girl friend who still visits me occasionally. But she also let me down when I was having a hard time—I turned to her for help, but she didn't want to give it to me.

It was easier for me to associate with boys. I was always around them. I think it was in the seventh grade that I read Jack London's *Martin Eden,* and I loved it. There was a Martin Eden in my school who was in love with me even though he was just a schoolboy, a real rabble-rouser who fought with everybody. I tried to educate him, gave him books to read. Although he came from a working-class background, I encouraged him to go on with his studies. Now he has graduated from the university and is working on his doctorate. Another boy left school on my account; he became an alcoholic—he's not a boy anymore.

I didn't know anything about sex, and my girl friends asked me, "Are you really so innocent?" But I've always felt that sex is the highest expression of love, and you can't do it without love—real, lifelong love.

Once I fell in love with a violinist who was married. I was seventeen and he was thirty. I never allowed myself to go that far. . . . I didn't have any sex life until I met my husband. That's the way I feel it ought to be.

Although we get no information about this vital subject in our country, children still learn about it, but in a distorted way, and often they "fall" early—that's one of our expressions—and their lives become twisted and maladjusted.

Although we never discussed it, I think it was my father who gave me the feeling that sex was the greatest expression of love and should never be abused.

So there's no sex education in school?

No, the schools don't teach anything about it at all. All the kids do is laugh and giggle. My mother didn't teach me anything either, but she also didn't tell me *not* to do anything. I've noticed that when a mother is suspicious of her teenage daughter, the daughter starts even earlier. But my mother said to me, "You'll get sick of the whole business soon enough."

What was your main incentive in deciding on a profession?

Well, I was a member of a literary family who despised physics, mathematics, and engineering, and although I developed a taste for those subjects in school, and for a time liked mathematics, these subjects were rather alien to me, since they were totally alien at home. There the typewriter chattered all the time; someone was always writing something, creating something. So I began to write poetry at an early age too, since I had learned many poems by heart and loved writers.

Would you have chosen another profession if you had been a man?

I don't know. Perhaps it's a way of excusing myself, but I probably wouldn't be in a publishing house now. Had I been a man I would have traveled around Russia, because I realize now that one has to experience the Russian language personally, intensely, not only secondhand.

I also would have changed jobs often. As a woman, that's hard to do. You know yourself how it gets in the way. But of course I would have kept on writing. . . .

Are there typically female professions in Russia?

Of course. Textile workers, for instance, are mostly women. Doctors and physical therapists are also mostly women. Almost all teachers are women. At day-care centers practically all employees are women. People who clean are usually women. As a matter of fact, most service work is done by women, at home and in the community. In the country women work mostly on the kolkhoz.*

Why do you think that's so?

Because the salaries are low—no family can live on a salary like that. It's terribly sad. Our women have a horrible time. They have to lift such heavy stuff in factories that it's hard to believe that they can give birth to a baby afterwards.

Of course prestige also plays a part in this. A man often feels embarrassed to do household or household-related chores. Here, dishwashers are always women. Teachers are also very badly paid, and that's why they're mostly women.

Do women have problems at work that men don't have?

Women aren't readily accepted in important posts. An employer can say, "Why should I take a woman with two children? What good is she to me? She'll stay home because of the children." What can she say? He's right, after all. If the children are sick she'll have to stay at home and give less time to her

---

* A kolkhoz is a Soviet collective farm.

work. Russian fathers don't stay home with sick children, although according to law they're entitled to their pay.

Could you imagine a man working at a day-care center?

Yes, I can imagine it, but one doesn't often find men suitable for that. Here there are very few responsible fathers; they all drink too much. A woman can't really leave a child in the care of a man on whom she can't depend and who may start drinking. That happens mostly in working-class families.

Do you like your work?

Yes, of course I do. Above all, I love the creative part. Since I write myself I also enjoy editing what others write. I hate technical work, but to write myself or to read and edit is a pleasure.

Could you possibly imagine staying at home?

Yes, if I had a rich husband. If I could write and not be bothered by housework. I have a lot of ideas, but it's hard to realize them—I have so little time.

Do you think that women and men have the same goals in life?

Yes, but I think that women are more honest than men. When Jesus was taken to Golgotha, women accompanied him, but none of the apostles were at his side. They kept silent for a long time—perhaps for a great cause. If they had also been crucified the Gospels wouldn't have been written. But the fact that women accompanied Jesus is symbolic to me. For example, in the thirties, when the whole country was a mass of lies and betrayals, the women lied less. Akhmatova* and Tsvetayeva were only "fragile creatures," but they didn't lie. They could

* Anna Akhmatova (1889–1966) was a Russian poet.

be broke, they could starve—Tsvetayeva went so far as to hang herself—but they didn't lie.

When we were forbidden to believe in God, the soldiers came to the villages brandishing their pistols, asking, "Are you believers?" "No," everyone answered. But still the women went to church, and it's they who have kept religion alive.

But I didn't really answer the question—I got sidetracked. It depends on what kind of man and woman we are talking about. In a certain sense they have the same goals—to travel, have a career, make money. But there are some men who look for a real purpose in life. It's fantastic when that kind of man and woman find each other. That's why I like Bulgakov's* novel *The Master and Margarita* so much. It's about what happens when men and women have the same goals as well as a love relationship where they share the same griefs and joys. I hate a Romeo and Juliet kind of love. I don't think it's real love. Love is a link between people who have really suffered, who understand each other without words, as in *The Master and Margarita,* and who want the same things. Then how they structure their lives is another matter. Sometimes it may happen as with Bulgakov: They leave this world together for a better one.

Is there a place for children in this ideal love? Can you envisage a life without children?

Definitely not. If a couple already in their forties haven't heard the sound of children's voices in their home, life is meaningless, period. Of course it's obvious that the woman suffers the most. Formerly, among the peasants, divorce was granted on these grounds, and I think that was right. One should have children, no matter how difficult the situation. Also, because of the low birthrate, Russia is wasting away . . . although I myself don't intend to give birth to a second, third, fourth.

* Mikhail Bulgakov (1891–1940).

Would you like to have more children?

Yes, but I don't have a husband. If I did, I'd have a second and a third. I would want a girl because they're so much closer to their mother.

How would you find the time?

I would leave the children in one of the weekly boarding schools. What else can you do? Tsvetayeva had three children, but she kept on writing.

You just said that the birthrate was low in the Soviet Union. What could be done to raise it?

To raise the birthrate one has to raise wages. They're so low now that women can't afford the luxury of two or three children.

What is a good mother?

Naturally, a good mother has to take care of her baby, take it out for walks and make sure it develops physically. But she should also give the child moral guidance—a feeling that life has a spiritual dimension. A mother who is concerned only with the child's health and safety is not a good mother. Of course she has to be a social being as well—she has to suffer the sorrows of her people. Then her child will turn out well. I'm quite convinced of that.

And how would you define a good father?

A good father? I know only one example of a good father, and that's mine. In the Soviet Union the father usually loves the wife above the children, but a good father ought to put his children first. When I was a baby my father always used to carry me in his arms at night. He didn't worry about his time, although he wrote a lot—carrying me on his arm. A father should spend as much time with his child as possible, and not only treat it as a child, but as an adult. Perhaps my husband would have made a good father, but after six months he was conscripted. He was twenty-seven, and it was his last call of duty. He was gone for a year, and I was allotted 15 rubles per month. When he returned, the child was a year and a half old already, and he was like a stranger to the child. Things just kept on getting worse and worse between us until we divorced.

I was much closer to my father than my mother, but I feel that for a son a father is absolutely necessary. I can't imagine my own childhood without my father, and I don't know what I would have done without him. I have a feeling that he gave me everything.

Do you consider yourself a good mother?

No, I'm a disgusting mother! I bring up my son on the run. I get tired of trying to keep him amused and give him a pencil so that he can keep himself busy drawing.

However, I do try to teach him the love of work. That's the most important thing one can teach a child—aside from spiritual and ethical values, of course. But I don't see these qualities in my son, and therefore I consider myself a bad mother. I should have taught him better.

Do you think one ought to give boys and girls a different upbringing?

No. I believe that girls ought to be taught to cook, clean, and do housework, but so should boys. People ought to be free and independent, but not arrogant. There's not really much difference between a boy and girl, except that boys have to develop more physically, and that of course is the father's job.

What are your hopes for the future?

I'd like to visit Sweden. Dreams . . . ? I'd like to write a book; I would so much like to write a book! About my life, from childhood on. Then I would like to take my son to the south, but it's very expensive and one has to have a travel permit.* But I hope to be able to realize my dreams. In the near future I'll get an increase in salary, and then I won't have to go to work every day and perhaps I can write my book.

You've been talking about the role of woman as mother. How do you picture the ideal woman?

The ideal woman is . . . independent. We have a tradition, which Chekhov wrote about in a story, where the woman adapts herself to her husband; he dies; she adapts herself to the next one, and so on. To me that's not an ideal woman. One must have one's own opinions about things—that's very important. I also think that that's very important in the role of a mother, but almost impossible to achieve.

A woman also has to be beautiful. Even if nature hasn't made her that way she must know how to make herself beautiful. If she then also has inner beauty, her own opinions, independence —then she is the ideal woman.

What does femininity mean to you?

Femininity—that's a very important concept to me. I even consider that without femininity, in the highest philosophical definition of the word, there can be no genius. And I consider that all geniuses—until now they've all been men, but that isn't going to continue forever—combine both a male and a female element. There's a lot of femininity expressed in Pushkin—at least I think so—and in Dostoevsky, too.

* Liza is referring here to a subsidized vacation at one of the retreats run by the trade unions, for which a travel permit of sorts is required.

What exactly do you mean by femininity?

I think that femininity is that luminous, essential something that separates us from the animals. Soloviev* wrote a lot about "the eternally feminine" in the most idealistic sense. Femininity . . . it's very hard to describe because it's so important, so full of contradictions. It's both self-sacrifice and independence, both weakness and strength—gentle and hard at the same time.

What impression do you like to make? How important are clothes to you?

We say here that people are judged according to their clothing and treated accordingly. So clothes are very important. I've noticed that when I go shopping and am well dressed, the salespeople are polite, but if I'm badly dressed they ignore me. I don't suppose clothes play a crucial role, but in any case men like it when women are well dressed. I don't particularly long for things, but I do think that clothes are a means of achieving beauty. I think women should be careful with their clothes.

I recently got hold of a pair of foreign jeans. I've been dreaming of getting a pair for a long time, but here they're impossible to find. My husband gave them to me as part of the alimony! He paid me with the jeans instead of money, and I accepted them with the greatest pleasure.

Then the other day I bought a pair of pants that someone had gotten in a Beryozka shop† and sold to a friend who in turn sold them to me. I'm terribly pleased with both the pants and the jeans. I never buy anything at all in regular shops. I scout in places where there are antiques and good used clothing for sale. They have things from the West, of better quality, more attractive, and cheaper. My husband found this shawl in

---

* The philosopher Vladimir Soloviev (1853–1900).
† Beryozka shops sell souvenirs and sometimes liquor, clothing, and other goods to foreigners. They are established at hotels and other places where people shop only with foreign currency.

a store outside the city, but it could only be bought with foreign currency.

I buy things in these shops because I want to be different. I don't want to be dressed like everyone else.

Are clothes expensive?

Well, I'm not all that concerned about money, but that's perhaps because I have parents who help me. If I lived on only my own salary things would be different.

To change the subject—sexuality. In our country there's a lot of talk about sexual freedom. How do you feel about that?

Sexual freedom? Well . . . I feel terribly guilty because the man I love is married and has a child. The situation is extremely painful; I want to break off with him. I'm guilty all the time. I don't know if you can call it sexual freedom, because even when we make love I feel that I'm doing the wrong thing.

It seems to have become more common for girls to have many sexual relationships before they marry. Here they even go as far as to say that prostitutes make the best mothers, and women often admit to being unfaithful. Or they marry a man without loving him for the sake of the children. It's incomprehensible to me. How can all that go on? . . . As soon as I realized that I didn't love my husband I divorced him, even though we had a child. I just couldn't live with him any longer.

Do you think that infidelity is wrong?

I feel that it's unethical. Why should it be necessary? We only live once—why squander one's soul? But perhaps the children really need a father. It's a difficult problem. If a father is essential, one may have to live with a man one doesn't love to keep the family intact. Maybe it has to be that way, but I couldn't do it.

Do you have someone with whom you can talk openly about sex?

I seldom talk to my friends about sex and intimate matters. But I talk about what I experience in my relationships. I talk a lot to my girl friends, even more than with my lover.

Do you have contraceptives in the Soviet Union?

We have the I.U.D., although it isn't used very much. Women who want one have to stand in line a long time. We try not to use the pill because of the possible danger to a future fetus. Some also use aspirin, but that's also considered to be dangerous.

But above all we have many abortions. They're horrible, absolutely horrible. But what's the answer? Our contraceptives aren't any good. There are condoms, but they're so repulsive and bad that we would rather go through an abortion. . . . The first Christians copulated only in order to procreate. In my opinion abortions are punishments for our sins.

Have you ever had an abortion?

Yes, many—seven. It's hard both physically and psychologically. Now that it's done with drugs there's no pain, but it's hard on the psyche.

How are women affected?

There are painful repercussions. There's no way of thinking about anything else when you're pregnant and you have to wait two months for an abortion. Then the aftermath is difficult. It affects not only your sex life, but also life in general. Sometimes I fear that I may be pregnant again; then I can't think about anything else, can't write, can't read, can't do anything.

People say that when a woman gives birth to a child she gets younger, and when she has an abortion she gets twice as old.

So I have become seven times as old! . . . The only concern doctors seem to have is to make abortions relatively painless. Previously no drugs were given. But the dread of pregnancy still remains stronger than anything else.

How did you react when you discovered that you were pregnant the first time?

I was hysterical. It was totally unexpected, since I didn't believe . . . I couldn't imagine that children were conceived that quickly. No one had told me anything. I got together with my husband, and I got pregnant immediately. It was so strange and unexpected that I had an abortion, though naturally I should have had that first baby. I went through with the second pregnancy and mostly felt fine, but I developed toxemia. The delivery was very difficult. They don't use any drugs, gas, anything. None of the women around me wanted them either. I begged for a Caesarean, howled like an animal, couldn't stand the pain any longer. I screamed so much that they finally had to give me something to induce labor, and I had terrible contractions and kept on screaming until there was blood in my mouth.

A friend had a baby two months later and told me that an old lady who had taken a three months' course told her how to prepare for each contraction. She gave no drugs, but only explained in what position my friend should lie. They also give massage, but that doesn't help. One feels like an animal.

My baby was born in a special clinic, but still. . . . During the delivery I was badly torn, but they didn't even sew me up. Recently I went to a gynecologist who asked me whether I had given birth in the country—but in fact I gave birth at a special clinic in the capital.

Did you feel that the pains you suffered affected your relationship to the child?

No, I felt it was quite normal. I knew that it would hurt. I was so happy to see him that I forgot it all.

In our country [Sweden] the father is usually present at the delivery. How do you feel about that?

I think it's wrong. I think women should be mysterious. I don't want anyone to see my pain—and that includes my husband.

How was the hospital? How many in each ward?

There were twelve in each ward. I was happy to be among all those women. One is so sensitive after a delivery—all of them were so open and receptive. They listened to me, and of course I gabbed on as usual—not about babies, but my usual propaganda. We had some lively discussions. I get very sentimental when I think about the time I spent there.

Didn't you discuss the problems of women?

No. We talked about literature and politics, very little about children.

As a woman, what do you find the most difficult problems to cope with?

My main problem is that the man I love is married and has a child.

I'd also like to leave Moscow and live in the country—writing books, working with children—so that my boy could grow up in healthy surroundings. But in many ways my child is dependent on my parents, and I'm also unprepared for a life in the country; I couldn't manage it. Besides, they wouldn't let me go, but I know I would like it.

Sometimes when things are most difficult I long for the presence of a man who is strong, a *bogatyr** who would shelter me so that I wouldn't have to think about anything. Sometimes I feel like that, although I consider myself independent. Espe-

* This is what the supernaturally strong heroes of Russian folk legend are called.

cially when I'm sick I wish I had someone to love, to cuddle up to, someone totally responsible for me. But unfortunately my character and my pride put that almost out of reach.

What, according to you, are women's most pressing problems here?

Their husbands' low salaries, and the limited time they have left for their children. Most women aren't wildly enthusiastic about their work; they'd like to bring up their children in a normal way, but they're too busy trying to make money. It seems to me that our women suffer from equality. I wish it weren't so, but men's low salaries make it impossible to live. Besides, men drink heavily, which adds to the problems of women. Here they say that when the price of wine and vodka goes up, the children feel it first. The more men spend on drink, the less is left for the children.

You read Baranskaya's **A Week Like Any Other.*** *Do you think it is an accurate picture of a woman's life here?*

Yes, I think the story is typical, very typical.

Is it also typical that Olga in the story doesn't think of making any changes?

That she doesn't think about change is typical, although I don't think it's normal. But that's the way it is: Soviet women are unable to look at their lives. They're happy for the children to have some kind of father. And even if the woman works and comes home laden with shopping bags and gets into arguments, everything is all right—at least she has a husband. There are others in worse situations—without a husband. Married women don't assert themselves and disdain women who don't have husbands.

---

* Natalya Baranskaya (1908–   ). Her short novel *A Week Like Any Other* (1969) describes a modern Soviet woman's week, day by day.

What changes would you like to see?

In the whole country? Of course I'd like to see wages raised, and I'd like to see men and fathers assume a larger role at home. They owe more to their children than twenty-five percent of their salary, which is the norm. They should be obliged to do more, and if they don't listen to their own consciences, the law should be more stringent.

What does equality mean to you?

Here equality consists of the women carrying the heaviest burden. I think equality is when a woman is completely free, when the man shoulders the main responsibilities so that she can devote herself to her own growth and development and understanding of herself. That's the reason we're all here. But here a woman's life just fades away without her being aware of it. She's young, then suddenly she's old, and she's buried without knowing why she ever lived.

Are you familiar with the women's movement in the West?

Yes, I'm familiar with the movement to legalize abortion, and women's rights, but where the right to vote is concerned . . . here all women have the right to vote. We don't need a women's movement. Here we're all convinced that everything is the way it ought to be. But I think when women were emancipated, it actually amounted to man's liberation from the family.

Is there anything you wish to add in closing?

Yes—it's terrifying when a woman speaks. The truth comes out, and the real pain emerges.

WOMEN IN
THE WORK FORCE

During the first five-year plan, which began in 1928, the industrial revolution gained momentum in the Soviet Union. The expanding industry needed workers, so it wasn't ideological as much as economic reasons that brought women into the work force. The effort to make women active in skilled labor has been successful. In 1928, 24 percent of skilled laborers were women; by 1972 it had risen to 51.5 percent.

In the Soviet Union the right to work has been written into the constitution, and officially there has been no unemployment since 1930. Equal pay for equal work is established by law.

Despite this, the Soviet woman is discriminated against in the work place. The same sex roles exist as in other countries; the women perform the service and routine jobs, while the men perform the upper-echelon and management jobs. In addition, the job categories dominated by women are supervised by men.

Women generally constitute the majority in light industry (textiles, ready-made clothing, the food industry), medicine, teaching, and services.

The following list of women's professions was compiled in the Soviet Union in 1970. The picture has not changed appreciably since then.

Profession	Percentage of Women
Nurses	99
Typists	99
Day-care personnel	98
Pediatricians	98
Secretaries	95
Librarians	95
Cashiers	94
Clothing industry	88
Laboratory personnel	85
Midwives	83
Telephone operators	83
Managerial personnel in institutions	82
Computer operators	77
Doctors	74
Workers in food industries	74
Teachers	72
Textile workers	72

These professions are among the lowest paid. A teacher, for example, makes 100 rubles a month as a starting salary and 145 rubles after long service; a miner usually makes more than 200 rubles.

A 1972 budget proposed for the Soviet working family assumed that the man's salary was 50 percent higher than the woman's—it was taken for granted that the woman worked and that she was badly paid.

However, laws do exist to protect women. Women cannot, without explicit reasons, be forced to work overtime. They can't have jobs that expose them to radiation. Pregnant and nursing women cannot work between ten at night and six in the morning. From the fifth month of pregnancy a woman cannot work overtime or work on holidays, nor can a nursing woman.

According to law, women have the statutory right to work part-time and the right to sick leave with various benefits if they have children under the age of two. Women with new-born children have the right to four months' leave with pay and one year's leave of absence without pay.

If one chooses to see sex roles as biologically determined, as experts in the Soviet Union do, it is possible to see these laws and the job segregation that accompanies them as protective of women. But it is also unavoidably true that as long as nothing changes in the male marketplace—and as long as men's role as parents is overlooked—the present power structure will remain the same. Women will continue to be discriminated against, the "aberrant" party in the labor market. As long as the government avoids a complete reexamination of the whole labor picture and seeks only to make it easier for women to execute their double duties as workers and as mothers, real changes cannot take place.

LYALYA

"A GIRL SHOULD ALWAYS BE CHARMING AND SWEET."

We knock on a door in Moscow University's enormous student city. There are about a thousand student rooms in the buildings that constitute the familiar "stalinscraper" on the Lenin Hills. Our only address is the number on the door, and without the help of friends we could hardly have found our way. The labyrinthine building—with its stairs, walks, and corridors—seems expressly designed to get lost in.

We are visiting Lyalya, whom we have never met. She, her husband, and their baby boy live in one room measuring 11 square meters, the space allotted to married students. The room is part of a two-room suite in which they share the hallway, a toilet, and a shower with a neighbor. The kitchen is also communal.

Lyalya and Sergei's room is filled to the brim. Besides the crib there is a small double bed, a bookshelf, a small table that also serves as a dining table, a desk and a place to change the baby, plus two chairs. That leaves only a few meters to move around in.

Lyalya is twenty-two. She is from Uzbekistan, has black hair and blue-black eyes. She is small, slim, and pale. During the interview she sits on the bed with the tape recorder next to her, her hands folded in her lap.

She speaks softly, distinctly, and simply: These are my feelings; this is the way we live. She is accommodating and gentle; she cuddles and feeds the baby as she replies to our questions. She serves us brandy and cake and isn't at all annoyed that we stay so long or that the refrigerator in the hall is off for several hours because we need the transformer for our tape recorder.

Lyalya grew up in Samarkand, but she has lived in Moscow since she finished school five years ago—the whole time in a student room. Sergei will take his final exams in three years, and she has a research scholarship. They plan to stay in their student quarters for another two years.

We ask Lyalya to tell us about an average day in her life. She says she breast-feeds, sleeps, breast-feeds again, cooks, breast-feeds, and tries to find some time for herself, which is almost impossible.

Has your life changed a lot since the baby was born?

Of course.

Does being a mother take a lot out of you?

No, it's not so bad. He's a good baby. Sometimes I can sit and read in peace and quiet. The worst thing is almost never meeting anyone I can talk with.

You feel isolated?

Yes. Except when someone comes to see me, I almost never go out. I've been to the movies once since he was born. Maybe I've managed to read two books! Before it was different. I studied, read, met people, went to the movies and the theater. . . .

How long do you plan to stay at home with the baby?

I don't plan to send him to a nursery until he's about two. So nothing will change until then.

What made you decide not to put him into a nursery?

The children in nurseries are almost always sick, and a child's first years are so important. He needs someone to talk to him. At the nursery there are so many babies; they don't have time for each one. At home there are only the two of us. I don't know whether it's the best thing for me, but when he's two, I'll probably let him go.

Did you ever consider not having children?

No, one has to have children, although perhaps not right away.

Do you think that you will have as many children as you would want to?

No. I'd like to have at least three, but we couldn't afford it, and there wouldn't be time and strength enough. I'm not sure we will even manage having one more.

If you had more children, what would your life be like?

Everything would have to be done more quickly. Worry about two instead of one. Frazzled nerves. Women here are over-worked. They rarely manage to pursue their careers, especially in research. If a woman wants to get anywhere, she has to loosen her grip on the family. It's either/or. To have a regular job and a family is difficult. Most women here work, but because they have to.

I hope to get a job—seven or eight hours a day. The rest of my time will go into taking care of the child and the household, so I won't be able to count on any free time.

For my mother it's the same story. Now that I'm no longer at home she doesn't have too much housework to do, but she works hard to make money because now that we have a baby she sends me money every month.

It seems that young people here are often economically dependent on their parents.

Yes, they are. It's the only way. We wouldn't be able to manage otherwise. We live unusually well because I have my stipend of 120 rubles, even though I'm home with the baby. There aren't many who live this well. My husband also has a grant—70 rubles per month. But he only receives 50 rubles because he was married before and has to support his child. Altogether we have 170 rubles a month for the family. It's impossible to live on that, so his parents and my mother help out.

How much do you pay for rent?

It's very low. Since it's a student apartment we pay only 10 rubles a month. But most apartments don't cost too much more. My mother has two rooms and pays just a little extra. Our rents are low, but our young people are dependent on their parents. I don't know of a single family where the parents don't contribute financially.

Only while they're studying?

And also later when they start to work. The older generation earns more than we do. For instance, Sergei and I will make between 105 and 130 rubles each when we start to work. It's not possible to manage a family on that salary.

How much do you spend on food and other necessities?

Let me think . . . the baby's food doesn't cost much yet. We spend between 150 and 170 rubles a month. Then there are such expenses as travel, rent, repairs, and dry cleaning. That comes to 50 rubles, so all in all that makes around 200, excluding clothes. Clothing is the most expensive item. Every year something is needed. Next year Sergei has to have a new overcoat, and I need a coat and a pair of shoes. A coat costs about 80 rubles and an overcoat for Sergei about 200. Shoes are insanely expensive. A pair of leather boots costs at least 90 rubles. Tremendous expenses, and on top of that one needs stockings, underwear, cosmetics. . . .

I haven't included a baby carriage, which we need, or a car, a refrigerator, or china. Those things are almost beyond reach. Our average expenses amount to about 250 rubles a month— perhaps 300.

How did you get your washing machine?

That was a present from my grandfather, who sent us the money. When I was a child it was my grandfather and grandmother who helped my mother!

Are your parents divorced?

Yes, they divorced when I was four.

Can you tell us something about your childhood?

I was an only child. After Mama and Papa were divorced I lived with Mama. When I started school I went to a boarding school because Mama didn't want me to be alone in the afternoons. So I stayed there until eight o'clock at night, when she picked me up. From the fifth grade on I went to public shool and learned some English. When I reached ninth grade, I wanted to become an art historian. In the eighth grade I had wanted to be a journalist, but journalism is a man's job; I think men do it better. I also lost interest in it once I began reading the papers. I thought journalists all wrote the same way. If one came up with an original thought, it probably wouldn't even be published. I finished tenth grade and moved on to the university.

Here in Moscow?

Yes, I studied pharmacology for five years. I didn't do so well; I spent a lot of time socializing with my friends. I was glad to

33

be away from home, and the ambiance at the university is geared to having a good time. But when I graduated I received decent grades.

The first two years five of us girls lived in the same room—and it was a small one! We were three Russians and two girls from Bulgaria. The first year we had a lot of fun, drank wine, danced almost every night. But after that it wasn't so pleasant. We began to crowd each other. The third year I moved in with a friend, and when she married and moved in with her husband I got a smaller single room.

Sergei and I haven't been married too long; we met after my second year there. The question was where we would live. The plan was for Sergei to continue his studies and for me to get a job. I did get one in Tashkent; it wasn't easy, but I managed. Right now I'm on leave and will be here for two years. What happens after that we don't know.

What does your future look like?

Don't know. I wonder about a lot of things. Our main concern is to find an apartment, and that will take time. Will we both get jobs? And the future in general, the future of the Soviet Union—will it be better or worse? That affects the child's future. We want to give him so much—the opportunity to study English, to study music. . . . The boy is the most important thing in my life at the moment. I hope that he'll have a happy childhood, and that I'll get a good job two years from now.

Will your husband also start working in two years?

No, he has three years to go.

What would happen if he got an interesting job offer in a different location?

I would try to get a job there.

How about if you were forced to choose between a good job for him or for you?

He would have to come first. That goes without saying.

Don't women have the same goals in life as men?

I don't think so. The women bring up the children. To have children is probably their main goal in life. Men want to achieve something professionally—in science, for example. I don't know the aspirations of a laborer—I don't have much contact with them. Male students want to achieve a goal within their profession, discover something, create something new. As for me, I'm not career-oriented. I just want to work.

Would it be different if you were a man?

Yes, I would certainly have other goals. I'd want to advance as a researcher. But at the moment it's more important for me to care for the baby, to bring him up to be a good human being. That means more to me than a career.

For your husband?

The most important thing for him is to pursue his career. But of course the child means a lot to him.

Won't there be a problem of jealousy if your husband has a successful career and you don't?

On the contrary. I'll be happy that he's my husband and that he's successful—and that I'm able to contribute in some way. I'm also happy over my choice of profession and my job. But the baby comes first; the rest is secondary.

If women and men have different goals, how will that influence the way you bring up your boy?

I don't think one has to make a distinction between how one brings up a boy or a girl. A boy is of course more adventurous, bolder, stronger. Girls ought to learn to dress, to be well groomed. A girl should always be charming and sweet. That's her role. But on the whole they should be brought up the same way. At least in the first stage. I haven't given much thought to what happens later.

What do you mean by the first stage?

I should think up until about ten years of age.

What constitutes a good mother?

A good mother—she's really the ideal woman. Interesting as a human being, well-read and well-traveled so that she has something to give her child. The most important thing is for her to orient her child in life, and in order to do this she ought to work. Then she must be beautiful—well, not necessarily beautiful, but well-groomed. She should spend a lot of time with the child—not spoil him, but show him that he's respected. She shouldn't force her will on him. Children ought to be able to express their opinion and be treated as equals.

Do most women share these ideas with you?

No, that's how *I* feel. I guess that most consider a good mother to be one who has a healthy child—and that's important of course—and who takes care of him and feeds him regularly.

What constitutes the ideal father?

He shouldn't feel it's beneath him to spend a lot of time with the child. He should take the child out, tell him stories, show affection, share some of his own interests. Of course he should be fond of children and help in the home, but the most important thing is that he do his job well.

Do you think the woman ought to try to stay at home with the children while the man supports the family?

It depends on the woman. If she feels that she would like to devote herself to rearing children, of course it would be preferable. But a woman almost never has any choice. There is no law that forces them to work, but if their husband has a low salary, they are compelled by circumstances to work. Also, a woman feels more like a human being if she has a job. Despite the difficulty of our lives, we feel that we are of more value if we have an interesting job.

Are there special kinds of work relegated to women?

Yes, most teachers are women. Doctors too. And sales personnel—almost all of them are women.

Why do you think that women dominate teaching and medicine?

I guess it's taken for granted that women are more suited to work with children. They're together with them more at home. And doctors . . . perhaps a woman's sensibility is needed. But things are changing somewhat. A lot of boys are studying medicine now. Most of them become surgeons; in clinics most doctors are still women.

Do you think that there is any advantage in women dominating certain professions?

I think that women are more valuable in the service professions because of their innate tact and sensitivity. But it doesn't always apply. Some saleswomen are very unpleasant.

Can you imagine a man working in a day-care center?

No, they're dominated by women. It's probably because men feel . . . well, men aren't known to have a good hand with children, especially small children, and they somehow feel that it's beneath their dignity. But there are experimental day-care centers where there are men who take care of the children. It's interesting, creative work. It would be good if they did more experimenting like this in regular day-care centers, but there the old system reigns.

How much do day-care nursery employees make?

Very little.

What about the other professions where women are in the majority?

I suppose that women make approximately the same as men. But women who work in day-care centers are badly paid, that's true. Saleswomen are, too. Maybe it's a fact that women make less than men. Being a chauffeur is a man's job and they make good money.

What does equality between men and women mean to you?

Men and women are different. To me equality means equal rights for the sexes. Same salaries, and sharing the household chores within the family. That's also equality.

What does the man generally contribute to the household scene?

My husband buys the food. I never do that. You have to stand in line; it's a lot of work and the food is heavy to carry. He also does the kitchen floor—he can do most things. When I need some free time at night to read, he takes care of the baby, makes dinner, does what has to be done. It isn't common for men in the Soviet Union to help as much as he does. Other women will tell you that. Women do most of the housework—they manage the home. The husband helps. I think that's fair.

You really think it's fair?

Yes, I do. In any case a woman can't achieve as much professionally as a man. Experience shows that.

Can you think of anything in women's present situation that makes their life better than men's?

No, I don't think I can.

SALARIES AND THE COST OF LIVING

The average salary in the Soviet Union is about 160 rubles a month. Subsistence is put at 50 rubles a month. In heavy industry, which is dominated by men, salaries are generally above average. A miner's income averages, for example, about 200 rubles a month. Within the branches of the industries that are dominated by women, salaries are far below average. The average salary in the textile industry (72 percent women) is 84 rubles per month; in the clothing industry (88 percent women), 76 rubles; and in the food industry (74 percent women), 93 rubles.

Outside the cities, salaries are still lower. Country dwellers are often able to manage only because of their private plots of land, the crops of which they are permitted to sell. It is clear that it is extremely difficult for a family to manage on one income, even if it is an average one. Families with incomes less than 50 rubles per person per month are entitled to a government subsidy. But to judge from the decreasing birthrate, people rarely choose to live at this level.

How far does a salary go? How much does one get for one's rubles? An average family's income is divided in approximately the following way. About 10 percent goes to taxes and dues, and 8 to 10 percent to rent. The rest is stretched for food. One has to plan and save for a long time to buy clothing. The Soviet government tries to stabilize prices; meat, dairy, and bakery products have been stabilized for some time. But anything that's not considered an absolute necessity—coffee, for example—has become much more expensive, despite the fact that the government maintains that there is no inflation. During the summer of 1979 prices were raised in restaurants, and beer and liquor became more expensive to buy. A common way of hiding inflation is to make minor changes in a product, rename it, and then raise the price considerably. Subway and bus fares are relatively inexpensive, but in 1977 the price for taking a taxi was suddenly doubled. Train and air travel also became more expensive.

A stark reality for most Soviet consumers is the frequent lack of necessities; just doing the daily shopping takes an enormous amount of time and energy. Even for those whose salaries are somewhat above average, the shortage of attractive consumer goods means that it is often difficult for them to buy things. For example, a four-door Zhiguli, a Soviet car of the Fiat type, costs about 6,500 rubles. But in order to make such an investment, one ordinarily has to wait from three to five years. The situation is different for the country's upper classes. Party and government members, executives, scientists, and certain artists and authors—often count among their privileges not only a salary way above average but also the opportunity to buy otherwise unobtainable goods in special stores.

ANNA

"IT'S SO DIFFICULT TO BE A WOMAN HERE. WITH
EMANCIPATION, WE LEAD SUCH ABNORMAL, TWISTED
LIVES, BECAUSE WOMEN HAVE TO WORK THE SAME AS
MEN DO."

There are areas in central Moscow that are not so over-whelming and monumental as the rest, old sections that provide a restful contrast to the huge gray concrete blocks of buildings and wide streets with heavy traffic.

Anna lives in such an area. When we come out of the subway we see houses of human dimensions, narrow streets, small shops, and huge chestnut trees that have grown haphazardly. We're in a hilly area with irregular architecture; it's a liberating feeling to find oneself at a higher level than Red Square. We climb a few flights of stairs in a house that must have been very elegant at one time. We ring the bell, but the door is open. Anna is on the telephone. She motions to us to come in. The atmosphere in the apartment seems to be a happy echo of spring outside. The one room and kitchen are just as over-crowded with furniture as all the other rooms we have seen. But this is lighter, more comfortable, and cozier than we are used to seeing.

We are invited to sit on the sofa in the narrow kitchen, which is crisscrossed with diapers on clotheslines. Piles of children's things to be ironed are stacked on every available surface. It's a messy, pleasant kitchen. Anna is busy doing something the whole time, and she seems

*to enjoy everything she does. During the interview she serves us tea
and cakes she has baked that morning, irons, makes apple sauce for
her daughter, nurses her, makes coffee, receives her mother-in-law
who comes with a ready-made lunch, caresses the child, and answers
our questions with great interest—everything with the same calm,
unflappable confidence.*

*Anna thinks it's fun to be interviewed, but she's also eager to ask
us questions. First of all she wants to know about our standard of
living. She wants to know about household appliances, child care, and
entertainment. Of course she's also interested in our clothes. She
scrutinizes us closely and later calls us at our hotel to discuss possible
negotiations concerning clothing.*

*She is dressed in jeans and a sweater; her thick black hair lies like
a rug to her waist. She laughingly says that it's the Azerbaijan blood
in her. Her voice is strong but at the same time soft and indolent in a
funny way, with a marked nasal tone. Large-boned, loose, and non-
chalant, she seems to laugh unconcernedly at most things in life.*

Can you tell us something about yourself?

I'm twenty-one; twenty-two in October. As you see, I already
have a three-month-old daughter. My husband and I have
known each other for a long time. You know—common-law
marriage. We've lived together for six years, but only recently
registered.* I thought it was a sad procedure, just a lot of
formalities. Not much to that, I think.

*Anna, her husband, and their daughter live in a one-room apartment
with a balcony and a large bathroom. Just as it is for everyone else,
the question of housing is a very confusing and complicated issue.
Anna has access to another apartment, one with three rooms. Before
her parents were divorced, the whole family occupied the three rooms,
but now her father lives there alone. Anna is registered there but
thinks it would be difficult to live with her father. The place where*

---

* In this case the word refers to the registration of civilians that constitutes the civil
marriage ceremony performed in the Soviet Union.

they live now belongs to her husband, who was married before and got it as part of the settlement.

Anna works as a hairdresser in a large beauty parlor in Moscow. Her salary is minimal—80 to 90 rubles a month, or 100 if she "works like a horse." Her husband is a writer and doesn't have a job. It's difficult for young people to find good jobs, she says. Competition is intense, and one advances very slowly toward the better-paid jobs.

How do you live if you make only 90 rubles a month and your husband doesn't have a job?

Somehow we manage it. Our parents help us. And sometimes he makes money, although not on a regular basis. One day he gets an assignment or a poem accepted; the next day nothing. Basically we get help from our parents. You saw how my mother-in-law came with food. Otherwise we couldn't manage. The only person in the family we buy apples for is my daughter. But I don't think the situation will stay this way; things will get better.

Are you planning to stay home a year?

Yes, I probably will, because the most important thing is for the child to be well. As long as we have parents, they won't abandon us. They'll see to it that we have enough to eat.

How will you solve the child-care problem later?

Try to find a child-care person. But of course one has to pay. . . . Both my mother-in-law and my mother are still young women—my mother is fifty-five, my mother-in-law sixty. They still work, and they don't want to stay home. They would rather pay someone than take care of the baby. But it's *very* difficult to find someone. And the day care here is so bad that the children are sick all the time. Of course there are good day-care centers for the children of ministers and other big wigs. But they are always full—it's impossible to get one's child accepted. The regular day-care centers are very bad—like everything else here. My husband, Misha, says that service in the Soviet Union is the worst in the world.

What do you do with your days now that you're home? For instance, can you tell us what you did yesterday?

Sure. Around seven I fed Dasha. Then I went to bed again but couldn't sleep because she kept on waking up. We got up at eleven and my husband went into town. Then a friend came by whose wife is in the maternity ward. We gave them a can of coffee. We didn't want to be extravagant, because coffee has become so insanely expensive, but we wanted to give it to them just the same. They're our friends, after all, and we aren't that crazy about coffee. Then it was time to nurse the baby, which takes a long time since she doesn't have much of an appetite. Then she and I lay together on the bed, played, laughed, made faces, and talked. After that I put her to bed and began my chores—laundry, cleaning, things like that. Then it was time to feed her again. After that I had something to eat and was lucky enough to have a half hour to watch television and eat in peace—which doesn't happen often. Then a customer came—I mean a friend—and I helped her with her hair. That took an hour. After she left I fed the baby again. Then I ironed. My husband came and left again. My mother-in-law and I bathed Dasha and I took a bath myself. Then I baked cookies and fed Dasha again. I talked with my husband, who had just come home. By that time it was two o'clock in the morning. That was all—mostly trivial things.

Does your husband help with the housework?

Yes, he does. For example, yesterday he washed those diapers. We do have a washing machine—one of the newest and best models—semiautomatic, but I'm not completely satisfied with it. It takes three kilos of wash at a time. We don't have that many diapers and we don't have the money to buy more, so we have to wash by hand just the same.

Who does the cooking?

When we have something to cook, I do it. If there isn't any food around, my mother-in-law brings something.

Who does the shopping?

It depends on a lot of things—when we have the money, if I have the time—but mostly my husband does the marketing.

How was it before the baby was born?

When I worked I did everything—cooking, marketing. Our parents helped then, too, but less than now.

What do you usually do during the holidays?

My father visits. He works, so he can't come on weekdays. My mother is here often because she lives close by. I see her almost every day. If my father doesn't come, we go out. We're lucky to have my in-laws two flights down; that's why my mother-in-law can stop by with food, and they're glad to baby-sit so that we can go out and have a good time. But there isn't much to do. To go to a restaurant or a bar is almost impossible. There are lines everywhere. You have to wait forever.

Anna's father is in the military; her mother is a doctor. "My father is a very conservative person," she says, laughing. "It's mostly turn right, turn left. My mother is more gentle, more diplomatic."

Her parents are divorced, and her mother is married for the third time. Anna has a half-brother from her mother's first marriage. She says she was quite spoiled as a child, even though she didn't see too much of her parents. They would leave early in the morning while she was still sleeping ("I love to sleep," she says, purring) and come home late. Sometimes they put her in day-care centers, but she was often sick and wasn't happy there. They got a woman to look after her; she stayed with them thirteen years.

Did you like school?

I don't know. I didn't care for it all that much. I don't think that most young people these days are interested in school.

In the thirties there were always meetings, everybody was involved and brimming with enthusiasm. We didn't get any of this. Only dreary Komsomol meetings that never dealt with anything that interested us. There are lots of things that interest fifteen-year-olds, but the adults always led the discussions.

I left school as soon as I could. I finished eighth grade and started nursing school. I decided to study medicine if I got good marks. I only needed one more subject to qualify, but it didn't work out because I met my husband. Besides, my marks weren't as good as I had hoped, although I did get a degree as a nurse.

But you prefer to work as hairdresser?

Of course. In my opinion nursing is a calling. The nursing situation here isn't good. In Poland, nuns work as nurses as an act of compassion, to alleviate pain, but here the nurses do a terrible job. They don't do their work, and when they do, they do it so badly you want to cry. They don't take it as a calling.

Why is that?

It's a matter of salary. A human being has to have an incentive to do a good job; that's what gets me to do a good job. I need to have my own clients. Nurses are paid poorly, and they have to do night duty and overtime because there's a terrible shortage. And then they have to do all the dirty work. Nurses who ought to be giving injections have to do such menial chores as sweeping and disposing of garbage. It's unbelievable, but of course the situation varies from one hospital to another. Some are good, but most of them have fairly low standards. The training is primitive, the very bottom. I played hooky at least half the time and I still got decent marks.

Why did you move in with your husband so soon?

I don't know. It just happened that way. I guess I matured early. We met when I was fifteen, but it took a while before we got together. A year after we got to know each other well we decided. He was married; he divorced his wife when we met. We moved in together only recently. Before that we met regularly. Sometimes I'd come here and help him with his chores, but I was still living at home. We've lived together here for about a year.

When I lived at home my parents didn't know about our relationship. I never would have dared to talk to them about contraception and things like that. I had an older friend who taught me a little. But my mother had already taught me about sex and menstruation when I was twelve. She used to bring pamphlets home, and that was O.K., because in school they didn't teach you anything. Besides, I'm embarrassed to talk to strangers about intimate things like that.

Which means of birth control is most often used?

Our Soviet condom! I only use imported ones—they're better. There are, of course, I.U.D.'s and birth-control pills. But mainly you can get by without anything because the woman has her safe periods. We don't make love every night. Sometimes I'm very tired, sometimes my husband is, sometimes I go to bed early and he stays up and works.

What do you think of abortion?

It has to be done when there's no other way out. I haven't had one yet. But that day will probably come, because there isn't a woman alive who doesn't have to have an abortion at some point in her life.

Although you and your husband got together so early, you were still determined to have a profession. What influenced you in your choice?

Mama! She was my only influence. She's very meticulous about her appearance; she takes care of herself. I think she looks very good. There may be women who look better at her age, but I'm judging by Moscow standards. Here people are very lax about their appearance. She goes regularly to a beauty institute, puts masks on at home with fruits and vegetables and things like that, and uses a lot of creams. And now she takes total advantage of me, demands that I do her hair, put on her makeup, all kinds of things. I tell her all the news. It was she who got me interested in this kind of work.

Would you have chosen another career if you had been a man?

If I'd been a man? I don't know. I can't possibly imagine myself as a man.

Does your job fall in the category of women's jobs?

I would say so.

Are there other kinds of jobs dominated by women?

Of course! Preschool teachers are exclusively women. Also beauticians. But I guess that's about all. Here women work in every profession, from tractor drivers to engineers. But I think there ought to be more jobs specifically for women so that there are *some* differences. In this century women have to be equal to men. Now women wear pants, have short hair, and hold important jobs, just like men. There are almost no differences left. Except in the home.

Do women and men have the same goal in life?

Of course. Women want to get out of the house and have careers, just the same as men do. It gives women a lot of advantages, higher wages, and so on. In that sense we have the same goal, but socially I don't think so. The family is, after all, more important for women. A man can live without a family; all he needs is for a woman to come from time to time to clean for him and do his laundry. He sleeps with her if he feels like it. Of course, a woman can adopt this life-style, but I still think that most women want their own home, family, children. From time immemorial, women's instincts have been rooted in taking care of their families, tending to their husbands, sewing, washing—all the household chores. Men are supposed to provide for the family; women should keep the home fires burning. This is so deeply ingrained in women that there's no way of changing it.

Whose career do you think is the most important?

The man's, naturally. The family is often broken up because women don't follow their men when they move where they can get a job. That was the case with my in-laws. They don't live together any longer because my father-in-law worked for a long time as far away as Smolensk. He lived alone, without his family, and then, of course, it was only natural that things turned out the way they did. It's hard for a man to live without his family when he's used to being taken care of all the time. Of course there are men who can endure, who continue to be faithful, etc., but for most men it isn't easy. For that reason I think a woman ought to go where her husband goes.

I'd like to have some household help so that I could be lazy all day—sit and meditate the way my husband does. . . . When he sits staring silently I know that he's working and thinking . . . and I'm not particularly good at that. But he's working when he sits there without opening his newspaper.

When we quarrel he says, "So *you* sit down and think and write poetry, and *I'll* wash the diapers!" But you can't exchange roles. Of course he helps me as much as he can, sometimes all day, sometimes not at all. But for women it isn't the same. A man won't do the diapers if he doesn't feel like it. I have to, because I know that there's no one else to do them.

That's the way it is. Women have certain obligations, men others. One has to understand that at an early age. Girls have to learn to take care of a household and help at home. Boys too, but not as much as girls. Boys ought to be with their fathers and learn how to do masculine chores.

What constitutes a good mother?

I really don't know!

What should the ideal woman be like?

She has time for everything and is never tired. She's satisfied with everything, even-tempered, and always pleased with her children. She gives them a good upbringing. She knows *how* to give them a good upbringing—something I don't know! She never gets angry but always explains things to her children. She quietly tolerates her husband's bad moods and keeps everything running on an even keel.

A woman ought to be kind and friendly, and an agreeable conversationalist, able to hold a conversation when her husband isn't there. But it's hard. . . . For instance, I don't know anything about literature, and the people who come here are mostly my husband's friends. I have hardly any friends myself. But I think it's important that a wife share her husband's interests. And appearance also plays a large role. It means a lot to me. I could never dress as they do in many families, in any old thing. I'm always dressed this way—not just because you were coming. I always wear a skirt or jeans—never a housedress.

What kind of clothes do you like?

Elegant! Expensive! Couturier clothes.

What have you bought recently?

A French skirt. It's hard to explain how I got it—not in a shop, in any case.

You like to dress well?

Of course. My mother taught me how, and for me it has become both a habit and a necessity. I'm going to teach my daughter as I was taught, and try to dress her in good clothes. It will be expensive, but I'll try. Clothes play an important social role here. And I like to dress well and won't deny myself that pleasure—and the satisfaction of feeling a bit different. We certainly don't have many opportunities!

It's so difficult to be a woman here. With emancipation, we lead such abnormal, twisted lives, because women have to work the same as men do. As a result, women have very little time for themselves to work on their femininity.

What was it like when you delivered your daughter?

There were seven women in the labor room. Some got drops, some laughing gas. When the labor pains started, the women had to get up and walk to the delivery room. It felt as if the child was about to fall out—it was horribly painful. I think it would be wonderful if fathers could be present at the delivery. Let them see how difficult it is.

What do you consider to be typical women's problems?

One problem is being able to find pretty clothes. Another is finding somewhere to go for entertainment. Either there are no places or no tickets to be found or no money to buy them with.

There should also be some lightening of chores at work, and the bosses should be a bit more indulgent if we come a bit late and leave a bit early.

What problems do mothers have?

What to do with the child after the first year. How to dress the child well. There is also the problem of illness. There is hardly a doctor to be found. If something happens on a weekend you can call the doctor on duty, but it takes an eternity before she comes, and in the meantime anything can happen. Sometimes when the doctor does arrive she gets furious if there isn't anything wrong with the child. The medical system is terribly managed, which is one of the reasons for the sinking birthrate. It's impossible to have children under such awful circumstances. Thank God my mother-in-law is a pediatrician!

What are your dreams and plans for the future?

I want my husband to get a good job—good enough that we won't have problems in buying clothing, furniture, household goods. I'd like to buy some furniture, but it's insanely expensive and hard to get, and Soviet-made furniture is badly made. Also, one can't get the provisions one needs in the stores—always the same items. And my salary is so low.

My dream is to have another baby, and an abundance of everything! Also, better conditions in all areas—at home, on the job, during our free time. To have a high standard of living —that's my ideal.

DAILY LIFE IN MOSCOW

As always where large cities are concerned, available statistics vary. But it is certain that close to 9 million people live in Moscow. In such a vast city it is considered a great advantage to live within walking distance of a subway. Many people have to take a bus just to get to the subway.

The Moscow subways are justly renowned for their speed and comfort. The air is fresh and everything is clean, but during rush hours the crowds can be unbearable. With bus and subway one can ride to the end of the line for 5 kopeks. To ride the trolley bus or the tram is still cheaper.

The lack of housing, which was an enormous problem especially after the war, has partially been solved by sprawling suburbs with huge prefabricated houses. These high rises of nine, eleven, and fourteen stories have been constructed all over the country on the fringes of the cities.

The minimum requirement for floor space was decided in the 1920s to be nine square meters per person (excluding kitchen, bathroom, toilet, and foyer). In new apartments the average space has been increased, but despite that, the average living space per person in the cities doesn't amount to more than twelve square meters.

According to Soviet experts, 20 to 25 percent of the population still live in communal apartments, where several families share the kitchen and the bathroom.

Since 1962 it has become common practice for business enterprises, institutions, and organizations to form housing cooperatives to build their own apartment houses. If one works for a rich cooperative that builds a lot of units, it's sometimes possible to buy an apartment in a couple of years. The investment is high, however. A three-room apartment can cost up to 10,000 rubles. In contrast, rents are relatively low in the Soviet Union.

The new standard apartments include a sink with hot and cold water, and a separate toilet and bathroom. The rest one has to provide for oneself. Most apartments have a balcony.

In the newer areas there are "service centers" with stores, child-care centers, etc. But many people prefer to shop near where they work. "The markets out here are mostly for retired people," says a young suburbanite. Those who can, shop in the center of the city, where the stores are better stocked, although in the suburbs one can often find markets with express checkouts. The old stores still use an antiquated and trying process that involves standing in line three times in order to get one's groceries. First it's necessary to get up to the counter to see what there is and how much it costs. Then one lines up at the cash register to pay. After that, one gives the receipt to the clerk who cuts a wedge of cheese or whatever else has been paid for.

To shop for food is one of the few household chores that men seem to share with women. The rest of the household work seems to be the woman's lot. Soviet statistics from the 1970s indicated that women do 75 percent of the housework. The other 25 percent they do with their husbands. According to one survey published in Moscow, the division of labor looks like this:

Chore	Woman Alone	Man Alone	Both	Others
Pay bills	47%	28%	13%	10%
Shop for groceries	70	4	18	6
Prepare breakfast	72	3	10	13
Cook	80	1	5	12
Wash dishes	64	1	20	11
Clean house	67	4	14	11
Make small repairs	50	27	6	11
Wash	90	0	2	6
Iron	87	1	1	6

S O N Y A

**"HERE WE DON'T LOOK FOR REASONS
WHY WE LIVE THE WAY WE DO."**

*S*onya *is twenty-three years old. She lives with her husband,
Volodya, and their newborn daughter, Lena, in one of Moscow's newest suburbs. Volodya teaches biology at the university. Sonya has studied French and Spanish and graduated six
months ago. She worked for four months before she had the baby in
order to be paid during her maternity leave; the job itself, at a mu-
seum, didn't have much to do with her education. Now she plans
to stay home. She is paid for the first four months and is entitled to
eight unpaid months as well. After that she has to decide whether
to go back to her job.*

*If she doesn't find anything better, she'll probably stay home and
try to make money translating; she'd prefer not to send her child to a
nursery.*

*Sonya has dark curly hair and looks very pretty in a checkered
cotton dress that Volodya made for her. They are unusually gentle
people, friendly and happy, and very proud of their little daughter.*

*Light and pleasant, their room faces south with a large balcony
where the baby sleeps. Everything seems idyllic.*

*During the interview, a few cracks appear in the facade. Sonya
continues to be soft-spoken, gentle, and friendly, but one senses a*

57

vague dissatisfaction, almost desperation—suppressed, but clearly there.

What is your life like? How do you manage on Volodya's salary and your stipend?

Without the help of our parents we couldn't manage. We wouldn't even have a place to live if it weren't for them, since we're not from Moscow. I'm from Odessa, in the Ukraine. After my father and mother divorced, Mama and I moved several times, and when I began studying at the university I lived with her and her new husband a half hour by train outside the city. The three of us shared a one-room apartment. It was difficult, so I managed to borrow a room in Moscow where I lived with Volodya. At that time we weren't married. We couldn't keep the room for very long and had no other place to live, since neither of us was registered* in Moscow. It's impossible to get an apartment here. But then my grandmother exchanged her room in Odessa for a room in Moscow. She moved in with my mother, and we got her room. The whole thing was very complicated. The room is part of a communal apartment and there are several people living here—a single man in the adjacent room and an older woman in the third room. Fortunately, she spends most of her time with her son, so that room is empty. But in May she expects to exchange it, and then things may get worse. Just imagine another family in our tiny kitchen where you can hardly turn around! But getting something else is almost impossible. First of all, we have 16.7 square meters, and that's almost as much as we have a right to. The waiting lists are enormous. We don't belong to a wealthy organization, factory, or anything like that. Our apartment matters are handled by the university, and they don't have much money.

---

* It is extremely difficult to obtain residential permits in about two dozen closed cities, either because they are overcrowded or because they are near defense areas. These cities include Moscow, Leningrad, Kiev, and Vladivostok, among others.

Sonya takes care of the child and the household now that she isn't working. Before, she and her husband shared the household work. She spends most of her time trying to shop, since there is a poor choice of goods in their suburb and the lines are unbearable in the center of town. The day before we interviewed her she spent most of the day trying to find mother's milk, which is available in shops in the Soviet Union, but the store that sells it was closed. Finally she turned to a neighbor, whose name she had gotten from a doctor making a house call; the woman had milk enough to spare, and Sonya was able to buy some.

Sonya grew up in Odessa in a large Jewish family. She was an only child and perhaps a bit overprotected, but she remembers it as a very happy time. She still loves Odessa and the surrounding countryside. When she was a child she dreamed of being a sea captain, but her parents—both teachers—convinced her that she wasn't strong enough.

School she remembers with horror:

In the beginning it wasn't too bad, but the older I became the worse it got. When I reached the eighth or ninth grade I could hardly stand it any longer, and I crossed off the days, one by one, on my calendar. Every day that went by was one day less of torture.

Why was it so bad?

You know, our system is antiquated. They don't beat us the way they did under the czars, but otherwise nothing has changed. The system forces us to learn things by rote, to study without understanding. It's very seldom that a teacher tries to arouse the students' interest in anything. Everyone is required to learn the same thing and think in the same way. And the hysteria over marks is horrible. Even seven- and eight-year-olds strive for high marks, and many are beaten if they come home with D's and F's. There's a terrible ruckus in school as well if someone gets a bad mark. The teachers yell and the students have to go to meetings and stuff like that to discipline

59

them. That must absolutely be the worst way to get a child to learn something.

We talk about her former job, which was a typical woman's job, and other women's jobs. She points out that all these professions are badly paid and that the woman in the family always earns the least. She seems to be very aware of the difficulties women have. Therefore we are a bit surprised when she says:

I don't think it's good that almost all doctors are women. Women are less suited than men for such responsible jobs. In professions that require special skills men are better. And it's mostly men who work in professions like that.

Why are men better?

The work at home requires much more of the woman than of the man. Women are always tired, but men have time to devote to learning, to developing.

Don't women have the same goals in life as men?

Yes, when they leave school many girls have great plans; they want to reach out, become something, accomplish something. But once they have a family, many settle for what they have. They may want something else, but out of fatigue or a lack of choice most of them adjust to the limited possibilities offered them. Here there are very few part-time jobs, which is a shame. One has to choose between working full time and staying at home. Of course women who stay home have more time, but their horizons become narrower and they become very introverted. So even if women have certain goals from the beginning, they eventually have to give up much of what they were striving for.

Men's goals are more centered on prestige and a good salary. In my family, for instance, both Mama and Papa wanted to get their doctorates. But then I arrived, and only one of them could devote themselves to research. Mama thought she could do hers later. But Papa didn't finish until recently. That's why Mama never had the chance to do research, although she wanted to very much, and had plans and ideas. But she didn't have the time.

Do you plan to let your husband's career take precedence over your own?

Yes, I think I will if there's no other way out. I've already started to think along those lines. I try to do more at home so that he'll have more time for his research. But I'm gradually getting irritated with things the way they are; he's doing something interesting and I'm not. But I guess it has to be that way in the beginning, if one has children. It'll work out. . . .

We both hope that we'll find some way to deal with the housework so that I can also get to do what I like. Partly, it depends on me to make it work, but it also depends a lot on the situation. Housework takes so much time here. Either you share it, and then no one gets a chance to do anything creative, or else the woman takes on most of the responsibility so that her husband can devote more time to his studies—become something.

Of course if she makes a tremendous effort, maybe the woman can organize her time so that she can do something else. I read in the paper about a woman from Riga who was a doctor and a professor and had ten children! There are some women like that, but not many. I can work a whole day at something my husband does in an hour. So it's different for different women.

The fact that women take on the responsibilities and pave the way for their husbands is a very serious problem here.

Perhaps people don't know *how* serious it is. It gnaws at a couple's relationship and leads to serious conflicts. One never hears women say that they got divorced because only their husband had time to write his dissertation, but that's the way it is. The frustration of never being able to do the things you want to do hollows a relationship the way drops of water hollow a stone.

Is this problem ever discussed?

Very seldom—almost never. We don't think we can do anything about these problems. We can recognize them and perhaps discuss them, but we can't do anything. Change can only come from the top.

What other reasons can you give for the numerous divorces here?

I really don't know. In the newspapers they say that a bad sex life is an important factor. That's understandable, since there's no information on sex available either in school or anywhere else. All the information one gets is from parents or peers, and that's only the most elementary information.

Most people get married very early, at seventeen or so; they're totally inexperienced. They have children immediately and become tired, dissatisfied, and disappointed. Before, this was accepted as destiny; now we get divorced. I have many friends who have divorced after six months, and sex was often the underlying problem.

It seems very difficult to get hold of contraceptives.

Yes, it's really difficult to get good ones. Condoms are used the most, but they're often of bad quality. A friend told me that there are already holes in some of them when they're new, and those that are good when you buy them break when they're used. So one can never be sure. That's how our little girl came to be. We hadn't planned to have a baby so soon.

You didn't want to use the pill?

No, I never wanted to use the pill. It contains hormones, and I think it must be harmful. I read that a pharmaceutical firm in

West Germany—or perhaps it was the state—sold pills that caused dreadful birth defects, and a lot of disfigured babies were the result, without arms and legs. I would never even consider taking the pill.*

So most women live in constant fear of becoming pregnant?

Yes, that's the way it is. Of course, some try to get an I.U.D., but the gynecologists say that you have to have had a child first, or at least an abortion. There are lots of home remedies. There are various creams and some kind of foam that can be inserted. My grandmother has told me that a little urine kills sperm. There are a lot of such primitive methods, but one has to know how to use them. I never could use any of them, so for me there's no solution to the problem.

Is abortion a solution?

For many women it is. Some do it ten or fifteen times. Often it's the only way out, especially since so many men absolutely refuse to use condoms. Then what does one do?

Did you ever consider an abortion when you become pregnant?

I already had had two. I don't want any more. I had the first because I realized that I wouldn't be able to live with the man I was with at the time. The second was after I was with Volodya, but at a time when we didn't know how things would turn out.

Was it difficult to get the abortion?

No, I had contacts. I knew a female gynecologist. I was given anesthesia and didn't feel a thing. But if one goes to a regular

---

* A number of the women interviewed confused birth-control pills with thalidomide.

clinic—the official way—it's a very painful procedure. They don't give any painkillers. It's awful.

She goes on to talk about deliveries. Not even then is anything given for pain, she says, unless one has contacts. She describes her own experience, how hysteria spread through the labor wards when some-one began to scream, and how it felt to get up and walk into the adjacent room when her labor pains began. She had requested to have her husband with her but had been turned down, for hygienic reasons, and she lay there unattended for two days after she delivered, because it was the weekend.

It's obvious that Sonya has read a great deal about the West and been influenced by her reading, and she agrees with the other women we interviewed that care in the Soviet Union is inadequate.

It took two days before I was allowed to see my daughter—almost three. They showed her to me when she was born; that was all. Usually they give you the baby after twenty-four hours, but on weekends nothing works. Also, they feel that mothers should rest as much as possible after delivery, and breast-feeding can be a lot of work. Since the pediatrician didn't come until Monday, I couldn't see her until Tuesday.

Could you imagine not having children?

Yes, I can. At one time we didn't have a decent place to live, and I didn't have a job, and a lot of other things. But now that she's here, of course I've changed my mind!

The economic situation doesn't permit a family to have more than one or at most two children. If one slaves away at extra jobs and doesn't accept bribes, one child is obviously more than enough. The day-care centers are another problem. I'd prefer something else for my daughter. The groups are too large, the rooms are dirty, the staff is constantly changing, and the children are always sick. A week at the day-care center and a week at home with a tense mother is the way it usually happens.

It's a horrible situation. At work a father told me about the conditions at his son's day-care center. The boy is three years old and his group is huge. To reduce the size of the group, the staff opened the windows so that the children would catch cold. I've heard of this happening several times.

We had also heard that story. Even if only a myth, it still suggests that day care is felt to be way below par.

Are these abuses discussed in the press?

To a certain extent. But always as if they were isolated cases where the people responsible had already been punished. The whole system functions badly, but usually nothing is said.

At this point we are interrupted by Volodya, who comes in with Lena. She is hungry and crying. While Sonya nurses her we continue talking.

The ideal woman? I don't really know. But I do know that I'm not the strong and assertive woman I always wanted to be. I wanted freedom all my life. I considered not getting married, not having a family, no children who would consume my time, a life in which I could do everything I wanted to—read, write. . . . Even when I fell in love for the first time, I felt that if we were married the love between us would die. My ideal was a woman who lived alone and enjoyed her freedom. But then I changed . . . no, then my life changed.

Everyone ought to find inner calm. In order to reach that, there has to be something beyond housework, something interesting, goals to strive for.

On the other hand, I think that femininity is inborn; not least of all, it's having a nice figure. I've always envied my mother, for example. Although she's over fifty, she's more slender and attractive than I am. I've always felt fat and wanted to be thinner. A good figure is an asset, but in addition to that, femininity is being calm, controlled, and having a friendly disposition.

It's also important to *know* that you're a woman—soft, calm, considerate.

Are such feminine qualities appreciated in the marketplace?

No, not particularly. There's no one who demands them of a woman. As a result, a lot of women lose their femininity.

You say that women should be calm and considerate. How do they act at meetings? Do women talk as much as men do?

No, men talk more. They're less inhibited. They usually know more about what is being discussed and therefore can have more assurance and drive. That's divisive. When I look at my husband I'm jealous. He can do anything he wishes—literally anything. He has a good reputation on the job, he handles people well, he writes poetry and even sews well, and he cooks when he feels like it—while I don't seem to have succeeded in anything. One reason is probably that I don't make enough of an effort—something I've never mastered.

What do you wish for now?

That my daughter grow up as soon as possible so that I can have more time to myself—right now I have practically none. I also want to find something to do that I really enjoy—something that will enable me to use my potential to the fullest. That isn't easy. It's very important to me that I don't lose my personality. All people are different, but life here seems to pour them into the same mold. I need to develop what I am, and to get to know *me*.

For you, what would be the ideal life?

Three things. To live with someone I love and enjoy being with. To have a job I really like and do just for the love of it. And finally to have the chance to travel a lot.

Where would you like to travel?

Out of the country! I want that terribly. First of all, Paris. I'd like the freedom to meet people—all kinds of people, not only Soviets—to find out about what their life is like, how they live.

Will it be hard for you to realize your dreams?

Yes, I think so. A lot depends on myself, and I don't have much drive and energy. I'm passive, and I love to bury myself in dreams and fantasies. It's as if I didn't have the force to act.

I have a lot of ideas about what I would like to achieve, but I'm not so sure how to put them into action. When I was a child I could do as I liked—learn languages, play the piano, read. But I never learned to take action, and because of that I suffer a great deal now.

Do you think that these problems are typical of women?

Officially, there *are* no women's problems here.

But what do you think?

I think that most problems affect both sexes. I may not have enough experience, and maybe I would answer differently if I were older. But I feel that all problems, including sexual and family problems, are human, not only feminine. Women's problems are part of the social fabric. If conditions were better, if one could work less, have part-time jobs and more leisure time, the existing problems would solve themselves.

Do women discuss their situation with each other?

No, because we aren't taught to think independently or to express our opinions about things and issues. We don't discuss our personal lives. We don't look for reasons why we live the way we do, because it still isn't possible to change anything here.

DAY CARE

In the Soviet Union there are nurseries for children from two months to three years old and day-care centers for children from the ages of three to seven. Some day-care centers accept children from Monday morning until Friday night. It is often single parents who avail themselves of these weekly boarding schools. Only 10 percent of babies are left in the nurseries, which often have vacancies. On the other hand, there aren't enough places for applicants in the day-care centers. In 1974 there were only enough places for 60 percent of all the applicants, and the authorities project that it will take twenty-five to thirty years to build enough centers to meet the demand. Right now, the availability of day-care centers varies; there are many more children who go to preschool in the city than in the country.

The quality of day-care centers often varies. Sometimes they are under the auspices of factories that may have very different standards. The number of children can also vary a great deal, as well as the number of adults who work with them; it isn't unusual for one adult to handle thirty children.

The cost for a day-care center is about 10 rubles a month. It's difficult to get qualified employees for the day-care centers, since the work has low status and is badly paid. A teacher for three-to-six-year-olds must go through a two-year course after public school; those who work in nurseries have no special education after public school. The salaries are between 80 and 100 rubles a month, except for the director (generally a woman) and the most experienced preschool teachers. Staff turnover is considerable.

The prevalent trend seems to be for parents to avoid placing their babies in nurseries, but it's thought that older children need to be in day-care centers—even though the general opinion of them is low and the conditions are bad—because they need a collective upbringing. It appears that uneducated women workers use the day-care centers much more than educated women do.

MASHA

"A HAPPY MARRIAGE IS WHEN YOU LOVE EACH OTHER
AND HAVE YOUR OWN APARTMENT."

M asha is twenty-three years old. She has an engineering degree and works as a draftswoman at a truck factory.

She was married when she was twenty and had a baby at twenty-one. Her husband is also an engineer. Their daughter is now two and a half and is in a day-care center while her parents work.

Masha was born in Moscow. She doesn't have too much to say about her childhood, except that it was harmonious. An older brother often took care of her when she was small. She continues to give the impression of a good little girl. She is dark, her hair cut to her earlobes, and she stands very straight. Her dress is a neat, dark blue shirtwaist. During most of the interview she sits with her hands folded quietly in her lap, laughing from time to time as if she were embarrassed to be talking so much about herself.

Hardly anything she says comes as a surprise. On the contrary, almost everything is a confirmation of what we've already heard so many times.

Describe your living situation for us.

We live in the center of town in an old house built in the forties, with a ceiling almost three meters high. It's great. The walls are thick. We can have the TV on without disturbing the neighbors. It's a big, roomy two-room apartment—not a communal apartment, although we live with my husband's parents. My husband has an older brother, but he doesn't live here all the time. I'm not saying that it's terribly crowded, but we would like to have a place of our own. But it works out all right, we never have arguments or scenes. Since we've only worked at our jobs for a short time we don't have a chance of getting our own apartment. Besides, our living space—thirty-five square meters—is so big that we don't have the right to sign up for an apartment in our area. We don't have the money to buy a cooperative, which is very expensive. Besides, there aren't any to be had. My in-laws have been promised a room in our building in another apartment, with neighbors. If they get it, my husband and I will move there in their place, since his parents have lived in this apartment all their lives and would have a hard time moving. There's a woman in the other apartment, and if we moved we probably wouldn't improve our situation, but for my husband's parents it would be preferable. They're getting old—my father-in-law is seventy-eight, my mother-in-law seventy-one. He's hard of hearing and always watching TV. He almost never goes out—just sits there staring. My mother-in-law works, and when she wants to sleep, he's still sitting there and watching TV. If we moved she could live in the other room and be left in peace. Our daughter is always in my in-laws' room since ours is so tiny, only twelve square meters. We have a writing desk, a free-standing closet, a sofa bed, a child's bed, and a small chair. It's really very tight. We don't even have room for a dining table, and if we had to eat there it would be unbearable. We eat in my in-laws' room, even though it would be more pleasant for them if we didn't have to.

What would you say a happy marriage is?

A happy marriage is when you love each other and have your own apartment.

What dreams do you have for the future?

First of all, it's that private room. . . .

Do you think having a profession is important?

I'd never want to stay at home. I couldn't even stand being at home for a year when the baby was born. That's what most women do. I continued my studies while I was pregnant, and immediately took them up again after she was born. My mother-in-law took care of her while I was at the institute— she wasn't working at the time; she already was getting her pension. After the baby was one and a half we started with child care. My mother-in-law got herself a job, since she couldn't stand being at home, and I couldn't either. To cook and clean all the time and never get out—it's terribly dreary. For me working is essential. It's so much more fun than staying at home.

I have a job that I like very much in the planning department in a truck factory. I have the opportunity to read and draw a lot. It's a small enterprise, so I'm more or less independent. I'm really very happy there.

I like to have people around me. In the beginning I was unsure of myself, but now it gives me great satisfaction to feel that I can handle things. Work offers a kind of moral satisfaction for me.

Why did you choose this type of work?

I really don't know what influenced my choice of profession. I wanted to go to a technical college. I had good grades in mathematics, physics, and other technical subjects. At first I thought of making a career in roads and waterworks, but my brother said that it wasn't suitable for girls. I wasn't qualified to judge, since I didn't know enough. Nevertheless, I decided on technical training, but at a lower level; there was no way my brother could interfere. I enrolled in the school and liked it right away. I didn't have a special goal in mind, but I liked the school. My parents didn't try to influence me.

For a while I thought about another school that specialized in economics. But when I visited it and read the brochures, the courses it offered seemed boring. When I decided, I didn't tell anyone until I had already sent in my papers.

My job isn't exclusively a man's job. Those of us who do the drawings are mostly women. The bosses and managers are men.

Do you think women's careers are as important as men's?

I think that the man's career is more important. If there are children, someone has to take care of them and be at home. Of course the family is more important for the woman than the man. Men are more adventurous, more goal-oriented. They want to get somewhere. I myself don't feel like being a boss or a leader of any kind.

Of course women have problems vis-à-vis careers that men don't have. If I could work continuously and didn't have to stay home frequently with the child, I might be able to get another job. But when my daughter is sick I can't go to work. Men don't have that problem; they hardly ever stay home for the sake of a child.

How did you find your job?

It wasn't hard. My parents have worked at this factory all their lives, and the children of employees are encouraged to work here as well. My mother is a draftswoman also, and she has the same training.

Here parents always help their children. While I was in school I had very little money. The grants are low—only 40 rubles a month. Mama gave us money, and my mother-in-law managed the household; at that time she wasn't working. Now we're trying to manage on our own. We pay much less for rent and food than our in-laws. My mother-in-law has a job to supplement her pension. We share the household work. Sometimes I cook for everybody, sometimes she does it. We have to arrange things this way since my mother-in-law works full time.

Let's change the subject a bit. Can you tell us how you learned about sex?

I don't remember how I learned about sex, only that the information didn't come from adults. School didn't teach us anything, and my parents didn't either. I remember that there was a lot of giggling and whispering among the children at school. But when I was old enough to be married I was able to ask my mother about anything. We've always had an open relationship.

I was twenty when I got married, although eighteen is the norm here. I was twenty-one when the baby was born. I didn't want a baby that soon—I was involved in my studies. It was hard later to finish them; I had two full years left. Also, I missed two interesting years when I could have continued living a student's life. But it never occurred to me to have an abortion. People warn about aborting the first child; they say it can be very bad for you.

I was a virgin when I got married. After the wedding we went on a honeymoon for a week and we didn't feel like worrying about it. Besides, we didn't think I could get pregnant so fast. But now I know more and am well prepared. I've become an expert in figuring out my safe periods. It has worked out very well, and only once was my period late. I don't want to take the pill because I want more children.

What are the most common contraceptive methods here?

I don't really know, but perhaps it's the condom. On the whole it's a great problem. Not too many of my friends know how to protect themselves, so they live in constant fear of becoming pregnant.

Tell us about your delivery.

My delivery was difficult and extended. I don't remember if the others got anything for the pain, but I didn't, except at the very end when I got an injection. I don't know if they gave me anything after that because I was so exhausted by then. My labor lasted twenty-four hours. I think there was a doctor in the ward, and probably an aide also, but I wasn't sure because the pain was so terrible.

There were five other women in labor in the so-called labor room. When my time came I called, and I had to walk to the delivery room. My daughter was born almost immediately. I wasn't allowed to sleep during the first two hours after delivery. They claimed that could be dangerous. Then I was taken to surgery to have stitches.

There were thirteen women in my ward and it was O.K. I was able to see my daughter the day after the delivery. She was completely swaddled except for her hands, which were bare; it felt so good to hold them. The next day I unwrapped the whole little bundle to see if everything was the way it ought to be.

How do you and your husband divide up the household chores?

My husband does the shopping, but otherwise he does nothing. I forgot—on Saturdays he waxes the parquet floor, but that's about all.

What do I do? The cooking, making the beds, and cleaning. The laundry isn't too difficult a job because we have a washing machine. I wash the baby's clothes every day as soon as I've gotten her to bed. But that's no big deal either.

I'm constantly on the go. I can never sit down as long as the baby is up, and when I've put her to bed there's always laundry and a lot of other things to do. I usually prepare breakfast and dinner for the following day. Then I look after my own clothes and do some ironing.

Of course my husband has more free time. After dinner when I'm busy with the baby and other things he sits and reads and rests. But we never argue about that. Since I have to take care of the baby I might as well do the other chores as well. . . .

How do you think children should be brought up?

I think it's best if the eldest child is a boy. If the eldest is a girl, she'll develop characteristics unsuitable to her, and her younger brother will become softer and weaker. He'll be spoiled, and I think that's wrong.

A girl has to learn to sew and knit. Not only is it difficult to get clothing, it's very expensive, and it's never what you want. My mother taught me a lot, and I learned some things in school. They have a sewing program for girls, and now I sew almost everything for my daughter and myself.

A woman also has to know how to cook. I love to cook when we're having a party, to really prepare a feast. I'm good at that, but I'm not terribly good at everyday cooking, which is something I really ought to know how to do.

Boys ought to do the heavier chores in the house. They ought to learn how to wield a hammer, polish the floors, and take out the garbage. I think girls ought to be the weaker sex. There are women who want to play the dominant role in a family and who also want to play a commanding role on the job, but I wouldn't want to be like that. I want my husband to be the head of the family. A woman should be gentle, tender —and lively!

How would you describe femininity?

If someone says I'm feminine I take it as a compliment. To me, femininity encompasses a lot of things—delicacy, a little mystery, an ability to bring out the attractive qualities within oneself and to hide the bad ones. A woman mustn't lose her temper. And of course she has to take care of her appearance. A lot of women give up on that as soon as they're married.

As a mother, a woman has to have patience and be loving with the child. She ought to put her child before herself. But kids like to kick up a fuss and then the mother has to be firm and stand her ground. I'm not very good at this. I don't slap my daughter, but there are moments when I become irritable and can't take it any longer.

How about the father?

A father must really be firm and determined. Not unkind, but he ought to affirm his masculinity. To the child he should represent authority.

Would you like to have more children?

I'd like to have two children, but I don't know whether it's feasible. If there's more than one child, the woman has to stop working. But in general our women don't want to stay at home. They've become accustomed to working in the outside world.

It would be ideal if a woman could work and have freedom of movement and some time to herself, even if she had several children. But then she'd need some household help.

Day-care centers are no solution. They give women the option to work, but no free time. When women come home they're still bound to the household chores.

I don't see how this problem is going to be solved, but some way has to be found to lighten women's household tasks.

I want to be a good housewife and mother, but I also want to do my job well. The workday could be shortened, but I'm not sure that would make a difference. No, I don't see any way out.

N A D E Z H D A
P A V L O V N A

**"HERE WOMEN HAVE FINALLY GOTTEN THE EMANCIPATION
THEY'RE ENTITLED TO."**

adezhda Pavlovna is dignity personified. She is the
most prestigious woman we have interviewed so far—a
Ph.D. and a member of the Party, she has been a university professor for more than twenty-five years. At the
moment she is teaching prospective teachers in Alma-Ata, the capital
of the Soviet Republic of Kazakhstan. When we meet her she is
taking a course at Moscow University and living temporarily in a
room in the enormous student complex on Lenin Hills.*

*Nadezhda Pavlovna looks typically Russian. Her face is round, a
bit bony, with a pug nose. Her reddish-blond hair is combed straight
back and worn in a knot with a large barrette. In a black tailored
dress and elegant high-heeled shoes, she stands straight and is rounded
but not fat; her movements are quick and authoritative. She is at once
imposing and motherly.*

*Her grown daughter, Ira, is present during our conversation. While
we talk they offer us lunch. A small writing table is placed in the
middle of the floor, and two extra chairs are borrowed. Our meal*

---

* It would be unthinkable to address a woman in Nadezhda Pavlovna's position by her first name alone.

consists of cold boiled fish with enormous potatoes; the fish is a catch from Siberian waters. With this we have champagne, and for dessert, fruit. While we conduct the interview, Ira peels apples and oranges, cuts them up in pieces, divides them into segments, and finally passes them over to us.

Nadezhda Pavlovna is the only person who really wants to know who we are and what kind of book we plan to write.

Before we explain, she is reserved and formal. But she immediately relaxes when we ask her to tell us something about herself. She is lively and talkative, and often makes us laugh. She's accustomed to thinking out loud and scoring points, and she herself laughs often. But she also cries at times when she talks about herself. Then she opens her handbag, takes out a handkerchief, blows her nose, starts laughing again, and says, "Well, girls, what else would you like to know?"

Tell us about yourself and your family.

I live in Alma-Ata in Kazakhstan. I'm forty-eight years old. There are four of us in the family: my husband and I and our daughter and son. Both of our children are studying here in Moscow now. I teach at a teachers' college in Alma-Ata. I've never really done any other work; when I finished school I was immediately assigned to a post at the teachers' college. Then I did my doctoral thesis, and after that I continued to teach at the same institute. I've taught several subjects there.

My workdays vary. Usually I start lecturing early in the morning; that lasts for four hours. Then I do the shopping, often at the open marketplace. That takes about an hour. I get home between one and two o'clock, have lunch, read, prepare courses. Then around six, the family gathers. My husband comes home from work and we have dinner. We dispose of the household chores quickly and then we have so-called free time. We mostly read the newspapers and magazines and watch TV. We spend an hour or two in our garden. There's always something to do throughout the year. If I can't find anything else to do I start replanting! This fall I dug up all the peonies and put them in another spot. This spring I plan to replant my roses, but first I have to take care of the strawberries. . . .

Do you have a large garden?

Yes, I guess you could say so—800 square meters.

Do you own your house?

Yes. It's a very unusual house, since we designed it ourselves. It's large: ten by twelve meters. Underneath is a cellar with a high ceiling—almost like an extra apartment. When we moved there I thought the garden was larger than necessary, and that the children needed something more. I got the idea to build a swimming pool, which my husband did, and the children learned to swim there. I like to swim in it too, even though it isn't very large, but it's adequate, and very important for us in Asia.

I make sure I have a few hours every day in the garden. It soothes my nerves. We usually go to bed fairly late—around midnight, but more often closer to one o'clock—because when one of us goes to bed, the other stays up and reads. Then the other stays up waiting and finds something interesting to read, and the result is that at one o'clock we're still awake.

My husband subscribes to a lot of technical journals. He's a geophysicist—a geologist. He doesn't do much fieldwork, but works out the methods for finding metals and often constructs the machinery. He usually comes upon something just when we're about to go to bed!

Some days I don't lecture but receive students who are doing fieldwork or are working on papers or dissertations. Anyone who needs help can come to me.

And then there are days when I don't have any lectures or meetings but spend the whole day at home, and then I try to write something. On Saturdays and Sundays we go to the mountains and inhale the pure air! In the summer when the children lived at home, all of us used to go. Even the dog came along, and we would camp for several days.

Were you born in Alma-Ata?

Practically. My family came there when I was five years old, but I was born in the Ukraine. My father was Ukrainian; my mother was Russian. My childhood wasn't especially typical. My parents were quite extraordinary. They lived together for twenty-five years, and my father didn't speak a word of Russian, my mother not a word of Ukrainian. It was also unusual that they joined up with each other; my father had lost his wife, and my mother was a widow. When they got married my father had eight children, my mother three. Then they had three together—including me. So when I grew up I had thirteen siblings—ten sisters and three brothers. One brother died in the war, another after, of war wounds. One brother is still alive; the oldest sister died. I still have eight older sisters.

While I was growing up, my older brothers and sisters practically never lived at home, so I was the only child. They were years of bad harvest, very difficult years, and we were forced to separate: Papa, Mama, an older brother, and I came to Kazakhstan. When my brother began to study at the railway school things became easier, because they clothed and fed him there.

What did your father do for a living?

He was a laborer—no professional training. The only book he could read was the Bible; he couldn't read "profane" books. He had to leave school in second grade. Mama stayed at home. She had never gone to school. Her brothers and parents said, "Why should we send a girl to school? Rich girls get suitors, but poor girls do, too." She told us that she used to cry a lot, but that still didn't get her to school. That was before the Revolution; things were different then. Maybe it was not being able to go to school that made her so positive and eager about our studies.

The war began when I was eleven; Mama was fifty-two, Papa sixty-five. And then it came time for me to go away to school. It was so hard to leave them—they were so old! But there was a shortage of teachers, and children often had to leave home and go elsewhere.

I went to live with my brother, which meant that our parents were left alone. Until then I had done most of the housework. They needed someone to help them get food, because very few can live on a laborer's salary. I made the fire, cleaned, washed. I was strong, and they were old. "How are we going to get along without you?" Mama said when I left.

When I graduated I was assigned a post in Uzbekistan, so they had to continue to do without me again, but they didn't complain. I worked for two years and then I decided to go back to school. I went to Leningrad to get my Ph.D. Even then Mama didn't say anything. So when women at home say to me, "Why do you let your children go to Moscow to study? After all, there are universities here in Alma-Ata. . . ."

At this point Nadezhda Pavlovna begins to cry. Her daughter says, "Of course it's difficult for Mama when we go away." To her mother she exclaims, "Mama!" in a pleading and urgent tone, and Nadezhda Pavlovna pulls herself together just as quickly as she let herself be overtaken by her feelings.

I feel that we don't have the right . . . to hold our children back!

O.K., now, I've told you about my parents and my formative years. Now, about the school. The town was a real backwater, just a little railway station and only two streets with houses. But I had excellent teachers. Because of the war there were a lot of teachers who had been evacuated to the villages. Our literature teacher had a degree from Moscow University; the mathematics professor was from Leningrad.

My husband and I went to school together from the third grade on. I think I had a crush on him even then. But we didn't meet after school or spend time together. Not even a little. We didn't see each other until I had graduated from the university. We were friends—that was all. To hug or walk with our arms around each other's shoulders would have been inconceivable, totally unthinkable! And I made him understand that he shouldn't even try to take such liberties. But when I graduated and he stayed behind to study, we faced the fact that if I worked as a teacher I would only be able to go home during the summer, while as a geologist he would be able to go home only during the winter. We were afraid that we would never meet again. So then . . . so then we had to be more open with each other. We got married.

When was that?

In 1952. I had already started to work, and he had just finished his studies.

Then the baby was born?

No, no baby, since I wanted to take my Ph.D. My husband got an appointment in Kirghiz, and I went to Leningrad to study. I could only visit him during summer vacations. At that time plane connections weren't as good as they are now. Planes were infrequent and irregular, and I couldn't risk missing my classes during the year. That's the way we lived for four years!

During the last year Irinka * was born. My husband couldn't even come to visit me when I had the baby because his field-work had begun just then and he couldn't leave. But he sent a whole expedition to me—my mother and his sister, who accompanied her. Mama couldn't read, and she was afraid to travel alone.

I went to him in Kirghiz when Irinka was eight months old.

---

* Diminutive for "Ira."

Do you remember that time as being especially difficult?

No, despite everything, I don't. Later when I was more mature
. . . I admit that it was a very difficult experiment. Naturally,
I didn't think so much about how hard it was for me as for my
husband. After all, I was in Leningrad among people and lived
in a student apartment; I wasn't as lonely as he. But for him in
a new job and a strange place . . . and the whole time he knew
that far away in Petersburg* his young wife was having fun! It
must have been very difficult for him. To his credit I must say
that not once during the four years did I hear a word of recri-
mination. "Everything's fine. I'm doing well," he said. Still,
he was only able to visit me once. There was so much work
that he didn't even get any vacations.

But you never thought of giving up your own profession?

No, that never occurred to me! In looking back I find myself
thinking at times that the whole thing was a bit foolhardy. But
there wasn't any other way to do it! Now young people aren't
confronted with such a choice. They get married, have children, and still manage to study. Things are different!

The most difficult part for me really came when I finished
my studies and went to visit my husband. He was working in
the country, and I stayed at home with the baby for about six
months. If I'd been forced to spend another six months like
that I don't know what would have happened to our family.
"What was the point in my studying?" I wondered. I cried
almost every day. It was only the certainty that it would end,
that we'd leave that place and I'd begin working in the fall, that
kept me going. Later I had trouble finding a job at one point,
and I remember a male professor asking me, "Why do you
create such problems for yourself? Your husband is a geologist.
Can't he support you? Why are you trying so hard to find a
job?" I was terribly hurt.

* Despite the official change of name, Russians often refer to Leningrad as Petersburg.

When he repeated that on another occasion, I said, "Your wife is a professor. Can't she support you so that you don't have to work?" We had a terrible falling out.

Your profession has obviously always been very important to you.

Definitely! When I was fifteen I never thought of just having children and a home and a husband. Never! I felt that kind of thinking was beneath a woman's dignity. I had a long correspondence with my future husband about woman's role in society. How I let myself go in those letters! My husband confessed several years later that he was more interested in the way I ended the letters than in the whole women's debate. But I took the whole thing very seriously!

Is work still the most important thing for you?

The most important thing for me is . . . our country. Of course there are people who express their dissatisfaction nowadays with . . . well, politics. But they underline even more clearly what this country, what the Soviet Union has done for me. When I compare my life with Mama's . . . then I know. Everything I've attempted has seemed to be so easy. My studies went smoothly, my career also. It was probably the right place, the right time, the right profession.

But the children . . . I was often sad that I didn't have more.

Tears come to her eyes, but she quickly composes herself while she blows her nose. "This ought not to be taped!" she laughs. Then she cries again and says, "My third child was stillborn."

Her daughter consoles her, and Nadezhda Pavlovna is soon laughing again and saying to her daughter, "Hurry up so that I can be a grandmother instead!" We laugh together and then move on to a completely different question.

What does equality between men and women mean to you?

My own situation is one of total equality. If one of us does a particular chore in our home, the other will reciprocate some other time. But heavy physical work is hard for a woman, so my husband takes care of the furnace. It's a dirty job and . . . it isn't my cup of tea. I always do the laundry. That's the way we've divided up the chores.

I think that all this talk about equality is something they invented in the big cities. There it can obviously become a gigantic problem for a couple to decide who is going to clean an apartment floor which consists of a few pitiful square meters. Our house is ten by twelve meters, and there's never a question about who's going to clean the floors. I do that. My husband makes the fires. He digs up the garden. I do the planting.

But doesn't it still happen far too often that the woman works more than the man? That she does double duty?

You probably know that a lot is written on that subject here. The "Knights of the Sofa" is what husbands are usually called in the articles. As I said, I consider this a problem that city people have invented. It's a problem for those who have no warm water in the kitchen, and floors that are two by three meters. If the woman cleans the floor and her husband sits around and watches, it's demeaning for her. But if one has a house, and a garden besides, the question of who's going to do this or that doesn't even come up. There's enough work for everybody! Enough for the children, the adults—even the guests!

Do you think men and women participate equally in society?

Of course. I've never heard of a woman not being given positions in the community because she's a woman. As a Party member, I've had many such positions. For several years I've been the leader of a political training school for teachers. We study Communist education according to the precepts of the latest Party Congress. I give my colleagues reading assignments, pose certain questions, and lead the discussions.

Non-Party members also have all kinds of functions in unions, as leaders of study circles, as harvest organizers,* etc. And women are active in all these fields. Our women are very progressive: If there are four women and three men at a local Party office, the women will soon take charge.

Bronfenbrenner † didn't like the fact that things were going in this direction, but . . . that's the way it is. When a woman gains enough freedom to participate in the community, she doesn't want to relinquish her position. Perhaps we'll gradually reverse this tendency and reach a more stable level of equality. There's something of a reversal going on in education. Official opinion has changed a little, and now schools are urged to emphasize the role of the family and to give girls an education that will prepare them for their future role as mothers and housewives.

When did these changes begin?

I don't know exactly, but I perceived it when I started to work in teacher education. There are different guidelines now than when I went to school.

How do you feel about this reversal?

I think it's correct. It's not at all in conflict with our ideal of the professional woman. They complement each other.

My husband and I have also had a lot of discussions about child rearing. Not about our own children, because it was obvious all along that they were going to go to day-care cen-

---

* It is a political act to take voluntary part in the harvest.

† Urie Bronfenbrenner is an American social psychologist whose *Two Worlds of Childhood: U.S. and U.S.S.R.* (New York: Russell Sage, 1970) is a critical study of American child rearing, which Bronfenbrenner contrasts with Soviet child rearing. The book is well known and appreciated in the Soviet Union.

ters, but about the problem in general: the woman, the community, the children. In the Soviet Union, we're falling behind where the care of small children is concerned. Not in theory—our principles are fine—but in practice things are below par. The nurseries at present don't provide the stimulus to develop that they should provide. But for a woman to stay at home for three years is no solution—she may end up staying home for good. After three years the next child will come along, and she'll have to stay home for three more years! If one has training in a professional field, one can't stay at home that long without falling behind. Women without education used to accept staying at home with the children—but no longer!

Do you approve of the fact that only women work in day-care centers?

I think that's perfectly natural. There's nothing for men to do there. In the regular schools it's a different matter. A teacher doesn't only tell stories, build things, and draw. Intimacy and closeness are also essential, but a man's relationship to the children tends to be more objective. If a man behaved in the same way as a woman, with tender caresses, and stroking the children's hair, the family would lose a great deal. The husband shouldn't assume that role. His relationship to the children should be serious and pragmatic—not so emotional. That way the child has two kinds of influences in its life—one expressed by tenderness, the other through a more objective relationship. We know that the preschool child needs intimate contact. But in the schools attended by older children, the practical, objective approach ought to be maintained. In school the real world is more important. That branch of teaching would suffer without men. In day-care centers they're not needed.

But if there are absolutely no men around in the preschool child's world, if the mother is divorced . . .

But there are men around! There are male music teachers and arts-and-crafts teachers and . . . men repair things, make things, build. Male images are always around. To the credit of our society, we usually manage to have people live and work in the same community. Here one can see workers everywhere, even in residential areas. So what would we gain by having men work in day-care centers? They would have to learn all the attitudes and feelings that a preschool teacher needs to have, which would mean that we had deprived the children of a masculine influence after all.

Preschool teaching is considered a typical female profession. Are there others?

Yes, certain female professions have developed within our society. I've never thought about whether that's a good thing or not. It isn't good for a teaching staff to be composed only of women. As for doctors, perhaps it would be better if men were treated by men and women by women. No, I don't have any opinion. It would take a lot of serious research before it could be determined whether that would be a valid change or not. It isn't a question one solves over the dinner table!

In Sweden it's common for the professions dominated by women to be the lowest paid.

That isn't true here.

But aren't preschool teachers very badly paid? (Ira giggles and interrupts: "Yes, and salesgirls, too!")

Oh no! We have a lot of salesmen also. Salary doesn't influence the choice of profession. Same work, same salary. Also, in many professions it's possible to work overtime and in this way to raise one's salary. Preschool teachers, for example, can work time-and-a-half, and receive time-and-a-half pay. They're supposed to work a six-hour day without a break. Many work nine hours a day and then they make a decent salary.

No, in choosing a profession salary isn't the deciding factor. There are others: the appeal of the work, the prestige. All professions have a prestige of their own. But I know that boys aren't enthusiastic about service jobs, since by tradition they have low status. And it's true that women try to avoid dirty jobs. Something that also greatly influences women is the possibility of combining a profession with work at home. I remember, for example, that when I was working on my doctorate I assumed that I would have children and so I had to have a career in which I could combine work with caring for children. It's also common for women to leave their professions and work in a day-care center in order to be near their child.

What do you consider typical women's problems here?

In this country? I don't think that we can point to any specific women's problems. If we're thinking of the home and raising children. . . . No, I can't see any special women's problems. Is that supposed to be the new fashion?

Do you know anything about the so-called women's movement in the West?

Which one? There are so many of them. For emancipation? *(She laughs.)* We don't need that here. We've already passed that stage. Emancipation is part of our style of life. I assure you that question isn't a problem here. We don't separate the women's movement from our usual activities, from society in general.

You have a movement called "Women's Strike for Peace," and we have a similar one. We also have certain women's committees. But they don't play a meaningful role in our society.

During the evening we ask about the low birthrate and the high rate of divorce. Just as she did with our questions about professions dom-

inated by women, Nadezhda Pavlovna avoids answering. Her excuse is that the problems are too complicated for her to express an opinion, since she isn't familiar enough with the statistics or analyses of the problems.

Finally we ask her if there is something she would like to add.

We've continuously shifted from one topic to another; I don't remember everything we've talked about!

You seem to be very much interested in social problems. I think that Bronfenbrenner has made excellent observations in this area. I like his work a lot, although I'm not in complete agreement with him that the feminization of our society was the result of losing so many men in the war. It's not just a question of the war; I feel that what he calls feminization is also the result of the conscious struggle we are making. Here, women have finally gotten the emancipation they're entitled to. Do you realize what that means? It's had enormous psychological significance! In the future we may have to modify our present notion of woman's role in society. But it's still too early to know what's on the other side of the coin. Until now we've only seen the positive side—and it really is positive. Perhaps the press is wrong in beginning to talk about certain changes. I don't think there's a question of women going back to the kitchen, producing more children, and bringing them up in a better way. Women will continue to have children, and women will continue to work outside the home. Nothing else is conceivable.

WOMEN IN POLITICS AND WOMEN'S POLITICS

Men rule the political scene in the Soviet Union. Half of the union members are women, but only 26.5 percent of them belong to the Communist Party. At the local level the women are represented, to be sure, but where the hard-core decisions are made—in the army, the bureaucracy, the police, and above all in the higher echelons of the Party—there are practically no women.

Out of 320 members in the Central Committee, 8 are women, which means that women have a vote of 2.5 percent. In the powerful Politburo there are only elderly men. Nor are there any women among the 109 members of the Council of Ministers.

There is no women's movement in the Soviet Union comparable to that in the West. The only organizations that exist are the Soviet Women's Committee, a prestigious committee centered in Moscow, and a fairly small number of local groups called women's councils. The Women's Committee has an elite membership and plays a foreign policy role, both receiving and sending women's delegations. The local women's councils, on the other hand, deal mainly with women's problems, operate independently of each other, and are located primarily in Central Asia.

L I D A

"IT SEEMS MEANINGLESS TO DREAM IF THERE'S NO
CHANCE OF FULFILLMENT."

L ida lives in a part of Moscow where there are railway tracks,
viaducts, factories, and bus garages. The apartments are old
and decrepit from "right after the Revolution," she says.

Lida meets us at a prearranged place—as usual, it's the
entrance to a subway. She winds in and out among the crowds so
quickly that we almost have to run to keep up with her. We are not
going to her house, but to that of one of her friends. We go to Lida's
several hours later when the friend's husband appears unexpectedly,
occupies the only chair in the kitchenette, and sits there with a dour
expression waiting for us to leave.

Lida lives in a communal apartment. Perhaps that's why she didn't
take us there in the first place. She wanted to avoid the neighbor's
questions as to who we were.

Lida's room is her whole home. In one corner is her bed; in the
opposite, a child's bed filled with tools, newspapers, and other junk.
Nothing except the child's bed indicates that her son sometimes stays
with her. It's hard to find a place to sit, and we have to clear off the
table to find space for the tape recorder. There are wood sculptures
around the room that she has carved herself.

Lida is a short, solid woman, pale and without makeup. She has a boyish haircut and is wearing a faded sweater past its prime, brown slacks of coarse wool, and heavy shoes. She looks tired and worn.

Tell us about yourself.

I'm already thirty-one years old. Some years ago I started to work as a chambermaid. I work between nine and six.

What did you do before?

I worked on geological expeditions, traveling all over the country. During summers I worked outdoors the whole time, and in winter I lived in a small room on the site. We made geological charts and did a lot of other things. Sometimes the work was very heavy, but I enjoyed it a lot. I kept on meeting new people, going to new places. It was an interesting life. But you get tired of that, too. I wanted to have children, and I had to create another life for myself, so I got a job in Moscow.

How do you live now?

I have a room in a communal apartment. Of course I'd like to have a place of my own, but there's absolutely no chance of that. It's a fairly large room—15 square meters. Only my son and I live there.

Before that I lived with my mother. But there's a law here that states that single parents have a right to a single room, so after a while I got this one.

Do you have your son in a day-care center?

No, he's only two and a half, so he's in a nursery. He spends the entire week there. I leave him on Monday morning and pick him up on Friday evening.

Is he happy there?

Yes, he likes it a lot. There are toys, other children, things that a kid needs. The staff is good and caring. But of course it's hard to see so little of him. I miss him. He spends his days with strangers, and when he comes home he seems to want to be back with them. People who aren't even related to him seem closer to him than I am.

He doesn't behave like a real son; sometimes he uses the polite form of address with me.* But in general things are all right. I'd never be able to bring him home every day.

What time do you come home from work?

I don't leave work until six, which means that the earliest I get home is at seven. At least three times a week I have to stop and shop on the way home, and since that's the time the crowds are the worst, it often takes at least an hour. Most of the time I don't get home until eight.

Do you manage to have any free time?

Hardly. I have to cook and wash and do things like that at night. But I do have a couple of hobbies. One is the theater. I'm part of an amateur group. It consists of people who are interested in the theater, both students and workers. We rehearse four times a week—Monday, Wednesday, and Saturday nights and all of Sunday. When we're about to perform we work as much as we can bear. Right now we're working on a piece by Mayakovsky.† It's a lot of fun.

My second hobby is sculpting in wood. I collect pieces of wood in the forest and sculpt figures out of them. I usually do that late at night.

* The Russian language has both a polite and an informal form of address, unlike English. Family members normally use the informal form.
† Vladimir Mayakovsky (1893–1930), leading Russian Futurist poet.

What else do you do on Saturdays and Sundays?

On Friday night my little Danilo comes home. My mother spends most of the time with him. She helps me a lot. On Saturdays I try to spend time with him—except when I have to race around and shop for food for Mama, the boy, and me. After that I usually take Danilo for a walk. Then he sleeps two or three hours. When he wakes up I play with him awhile, although he's very independent and spends most of his time drawing or looking at his picture books. He loves his books and recites his own stories to go along with the pictures. He isn't terribly interested in playing, but prefers to draw—he calls it writing letters. He doesn't care about toys, even his bicycle. But he loves to iron and do other female jobs. He loves to do the dishes, clean floors, and do the washing. I only wish I were as energetic as he! It's the same thing at his nursery. They tell him that if he eats everything up he can do the dishes—and so he eats everything up!

Do they learn to do dishes and things like that in nursery school?

No, he learned that at home. He imitates Grandma. He behaves like a girl, doesn't play boys' games, and at nursery school spends most of his time with the girls.

Would you like him to behave more like a boy?

Of course. I wanted to have a boy above everything else; I couldn't even imagine having a girl. I've always been a tomboy, and I wanted my son to have the same experiences and interests as I did. A boy can go along on expeditions in the woods and things like that. A girl needs more tenderness; she has to be taught to be feminine. Given my nature, that's something I couldn't do.

What is femininity, in your opinion?

That's hard to say. A girl has to be more gentle. Or kinder. How can I express it? Boys are easier in almost every way.

A boy should be manly, courageous, bold. I hope to teach my boy to fight so that he can defend himself. I hope very much that he'll learn how to dance, so that he won't be embarrassed at dances; I'd like him to join a dance club when he's older. The most important thing is that he not become a sissy.

Do you often have conferences with the nursery school staff about Danilo?

Yes, I talk to both Danilo and the teachers. He's especially fond of one teacher, who tells me what he's been talking about. He's generally calm and quiet and doesn't seem to say very much. But he has said some things that don't sit right with me.

Sometimes he makes up a lot of stories. He doesn't have a father, and of course the other children ask him about that. To begin with, he said that his father was on a business trip, but then he changed his story and said that his father was dead and buried. That wasn't such a dumb thing to say, even though I'll have to explain the situation some day.

Are you divorced?

I was never married. I wanted to have a child, not a family. I'm not the kind of woman who fits easily into marriage.

What do you mean by that?

I've always been more comfortable with boys and never developed my feminine side, so living with a man wouldn't exactly suit me.

How were you brought up?

I didn't have a father either; I lived with Mama all my life. I have no siblings and not too many other relatives. The ones I have I almost never see. They're better off than I am, and it isn't really very pleasant to visit them.

How do you remember your childhood?

Well, all I remember is that I was born after the war and in Moscow. That's considered lucky because I could get everything a child needs. Schools and theaters and movies and exhibitions—I had it all when I was little. We had a Christmas tree and everything.

On the other hand, it wasn't easy, materially speaking. Mama worked in a factory; she greased motor parts with chemicals and oil. She came home completely exhausted. . . . You can understand how it is when a woman comes from work totally knocked out and has all the housework staring her in the face. Mama had trouble with one leg, and that made it even harder for her. On top of that she had a sick sister to take care of all during my childhood. We never had enough money when I was little; we had an awful time. Mama and I had to go around and clean people's floors. It was terrible, but she gave me everything she could.

Were you lonesome?

Yes. Until I was eleven all I had was that sick aunt whom I didn't like—I was afraid of her. But once she was gone things were better.

Did she live with you?

Yes, the three of us lived in one room. It wasn't easy, especially since I was a tomboy and made a lot of noise. But I've always liked my mother and understood that when she screamed at me it was because she was tired. She always helped me a lot.

What kind of education do you have?

Ten years in school. I tried to go further but it didn't work. I didn't get into the school I wanted, and besides that I was working and didn't really have any time to study. My job was exhausting. I sorted mail in the evenings when I was going to school, in order to help at home.

When you went to school, did you have any plans as to what you wanted to do?

Sure. I've always been drawn to the sea, and when I was young I dreamed of being, if not a sea captain, at least a seaman. If only I could be at sea it didn't matter if I was a cook, a sailor, or whatever. I tried to realize my dream; I thought that if I could reach the sea I'd find some way of getting on board a ship. Of course, I failed. I was sent back home without ever having reached the sea. I didn't have a ticket or a travel permit.

What influenced your choice of profession?

Nothing. The life I lived was so splintered, I didn't know what I wanted or how to make anything happen. All I knew was that I wanted to go to sea. And I only wanted that because I really always wanted to be a boy, I always knew that.

In school I said that I wanted to be a geologist, but I was told that it was better to be a geophysicist. But that didn't have anything to do with what I was dreaming about. It was the taiga,* the campfires, and the other romantic stuff that attracted me.

When I left school I didn't have any idea what to do. So finally I applied to a geological institute, but they didn't accept

* The vast evergreen forests in Siberia and other subarctic regions.

girls except as reserves. They said that girls would eventually have families, and a woman with a family couldn't be a real geologist.

Since I wasn't accepted, I had to find something else. I didn't know where to turn to find a job, and I didn't have a soul to ask or consult.

Finally I enrolled in a trade school to learn lathe work, a two-year course. There were only boys. I did O.K. even though I didn't exactly love it. I liked the work, but it was a strain to be the only girl. My group wasn't too happy to have me around, and the fact that I did well didn't help any.

But when I learned to parachute I became friends with the guys in school. Then there was a horrible accident at the factory and I began to be afraid of the lathe.

So I gradually came to the conclusion that the job wasn't suitable for a woman. A woman has to be careful of her nails, have clean hands. But someone who works on a lathe gets coarse hands and black nails. They say that one ought to be proud of hands that show signs of hard work, but I was always ashamed of mine and tried to hide them when I was in the subway. I couldn't manage the physical side of it either—I had to be on my feet the whole time, and there was the noise of the machines and the dirt and the constant scratches, small wounds, and burns. It's not a woman's job, so I decided to quit.

At the same time I decided to leave Moscow. I wanted to see something else, change my life. I took off and landed in Siberia. Of course it was hard in the beginning. The life there was totally different from Moscow, not so comfortable as here. I did construction work. I liked it; it was interesting in many ways. But I didn't have much in the way of a social life up there. From time to time they arranged a dance, which usually wasn't much fun. People came in their work clothes and danced in a tiny crowded room. You aren't too anxious to dance after carrying bricks the whole day. They tried to organize other things like parachuting; they even had an instructor.

I also worked as an editorial assistant on the local newspaper and was in the local union.

Then my dream finally came true. I was invited to join a geological expedition that summer. I was overjoyed! It was fantastic! I loved it—for three years I worked in different places in the taiga. They say that once you've been in the taiga, you always miss it. I still miss it a lot, especially in the springtime. The forest and the smells, totally wild and untouched—it's impossible to describe how wonderful it is. To meet a bear . . . And the people who work there are so enthusiastic, so crazy, so optimistic, that you just can't get bored. I'd love to go back, but I have Danilo, and I don't dare leave my job here.

Would things have been different for you had you been a man?

Definitely. Men have more choices. They can leave home and move around more easily. No matter where a woman goes she's looked upon as a woman, and people ask, "What use are you? You'll have kids and not be able to work as much as a man!" That's the way it is, here in Moscow as well.

Are there any typical women's jobs?

Sure. Many. Typing is a typical woman's profession. Drafting, secretarial work, and most teachers are women. Also office workers, doctors, sales personnel.

Why is that?

Because . . . there are jobs that don't suit men—easy jobs, women's jobs.

Is it good or bad that there are special women's jobs?

Of course it's good!

Do you also approve of the fact that most teachers and all day-care personnel are women?

In nurseries and day-care centers women are more suited to dealing with small children than men. But where teachers are concerned, I think men are better; children listen more to men. They're always drawn more to strong people than to weak ones.

Do women and men have the same goals in life?

Hardly. They can have similar goals—a good job, a family—but not identical goals. Women often pin their goals and expectations on men; they try to get a good life through them.

Do women have difficulties in the working world that men don't have?

Yes. If a job involves travel, a woman has a hard time getting it. Strenuous work is also hard for women to get. They can't manage heavy work in the same way men can. It can hurt them.

What role does work play in your life?

It allows me to support myself and survive. If I didn't work I couldn't manage. Of course there are other ways. One can marry someone who makes a good living and live off his money. But if that way out doesn't exist, and if one doesn't want to steal, there's nothing left but work. But I'd like to have a job that really interested me—a job I did because I liked it. That's hard to find. But just to sit at home with a child would be horrible—terribly difficult.

What should be done to raise the birthrate here?

God only knows. At the present time it's dropping instead of rising. It'll take a long time before there's any change. The way things are here it's almost impossible to support even one child. To buy clothes for a small child like Danilo costs a lot of money since he keeps on growing, not by the day but by the hour. Food for a kid is also very expensive. He needs things that you have to stand in line for, things that you have to use a lot of energy to get. He needs vitamins, and it's almost impossible to buy oranges and things like that if you work all day. It's also hard to get fresh milk; there's a great shortage of milk products here. These kinds of things make it practically impossible to have more than one child. Having a second one is rarely done on purpose—usually it happens only if a woman doesn't want an abortion. . . .

Have you had an abortion?

Yes, once. It was terrible. But what could I do?

How about other contraceptive methods?

The only thing I know is the condom. Then there are diaphragms and the pill. But they're all dangerous to women. I think it's the man's job to protect the woman. But they don't always do it. Women are always afraid of getting pregnant. I know that when I'm with a man, that's practically the only thing I think about. Abortion is horrible, and giving birth to any more children is impossible. Especially for people like me who don't have husbands, just casual relationships.

How was your delivery?

Incredibly easy—perhaps because I wanted a baby so badly. Everyone was envious. The pregnancy was also easy. I could ski and was as active as usual the whole time. That probably influenced the delivery. But I saw how the other women suffered. The midwives hardly helped them at all, and they didn't get anything to ease their pain. It was horrible to see how they suffered, but I also thought it was humiliating to give birth without anyone caring about me. When my labor pains began, I went into the room where you give birth, and they left me there. At one point someone came in to get something, and she said, "Oh, you can see the baby already." She ran for help. But he could have fallen out—anything. Then a lot of people appeared, but that's only because she happened to come in at the right moment.

Was it because a lot of women happened to be giving birth just then?

Not at all! Next to me was a girl who had given birth to twins that morning—one was stillborn. We were the only ones there. I fell asleep, and when I woke up she was lying there with the surviving baby, not quite up to snuff, but all right. Before my delivery they took her away, so I was really the only patient. I don't know what it's like in other places, but that was a humiliating experience. After the delivery I had to walk to my ward, although one isn't supposed to get up immediately.

When I had gotten myself into bed in the ward, happy that I had had a boy, a woman came by and asked me what the child was. "A boy," I told her. "Poor thing," she said. "He just died." I rushed to the nursery and there he was, very much alive. They threw me out, but later the pediatrician told me that the child was exceptionally strong and energetic and hadn't cried once.

Would you like to have another child?

No, one child is what I wanted, a boy. If I had had triplets it would have been fine, because with three children I would have been entitled to my own apartment. With only one baby I don't have a chance of that. But I never want to go through that suffering again.

What do you think a mother should be?

A good mother ought to be able to bring up her child and educate him. She shouldn't ignore anything that concerns her child, but should not be so blind in her love that she gives up everything without thinking of herself. She should be able to take care of herself and be active in the community. A good mother never lets anger flare up but controls herself, even if it's very hard. She should also be kind, gentle, and good. She should have style. She absolutely shouldn't show the bad aspects of her character to her child, even if she has some.

A father should be good to the child and the mother, good and strong. But he should also expect things from them. It's important that the child feel his strength and his authority.

Do you think that boys and girls should be brought up in the same way?

No, absolutely not. A boy should be brought up to be brave and strong—especially strong—and to have stamina. He shouldn't be coddled. But he must also learn to be kind, he must learn to be good to animals as well as to human beings. He must not develop into an egoist; that's one of the most important things for a boy.

Still, he has to have a kind of protective shell around him, especially in his work. From very, very early on he must be made to do everything and learn to be independent. That's much more important for a boy than for a girl. A girl, of course, can be spoiled with toys and finery and clothes. She has to learn from the beginning to be well-groomed, kind, charming, and graceful. And if a boy should be made to learn how to fight, a girl has to be prevented from learning. Girls should not fight and quarrel.

Why should it be that way?

Because the very concept of a girl, a woman, is kindness and gentleness. A girl who fights with boys will be treated like a boy. It'll make her hard and influence her all her adult life. She loses her femininity, and no matter how pretty she may be later on, her hardness will frighten the boys away.

But wouldn't girls profit from being a little more "masculine," more daring, and tougher in the working world?

No, why? Our women are sufficiently masculine that they manage quite well.

Turning back to children—you seem to be satisfied with your son's nursery.

Yes, the one where he is now. He was in another one before that, and it was horrible. One day I took him out of there and told them I was never going to send him back. But later it was almost impossible to find another place for him.

The fact is that a lot of nursery personnel seem to judge people according to the way they're dressed. Once when I came in my ugly clothes the people in charge said that unfortunately there was no place, even though I was at the head of the list. Then another woman came in dressed in a fur coat, and they offered her caramels and said that of course she could enroll her child. Things like that happened to me several times.

Danilo was kicked around like a football until I finally got him in where he is now. Later on, when he's three, he'll start at the day-care center, probably a hell of a long way away. Then he'll have to be awakened early, force-fed when he's so tired he can hardly open his mouth, and dragged around in trams and buses bursting with people who are hurrying to their jobs. He'll catch the flu, because everyone around him will be coughing. It'll be crowded, people will be screaming at each other, and he'll have to listen to all of that. Then, when he gets to the day-care center, it'll be the same thing all over again. The adults behave like pigs. They yell at the children and use coarse language. And of course the children repeat everything they hear.

So clearly adults are seldom able to act the way they should toward children?

These days it's practically impossible. But if a woman is happy in her work and with her husband, her family, and her standard of living, then she can be a good woman. If she doesn't have to worry about being supported, if she knows she'll see the man she loves and her child when she comes home, and if perhaps her husband has bought flowers or theater tickets for her, and her child has come home with good marks, then she can be in a good mood. If she has a happy private life she can develop her femininity completely. But women like that are hard to come by.

An ideal woman is one who can handle herself in all social situations, who knows how to take care of herself and her family, and who can hide her fatigue in front of other family members, especially in front of her husband. Of course a sensitive man would see that she was tired and help her. But she should try to hide her fatigue and to be happy and active intellectually so that it's always interesting to talk to her.

You say that a husband ought to help his wife when she's tired. How do you think household work should be divided?

If I were married I would make absolutely sure that my husband never saw me washing. I would wash when he was out, or else early in the morning when he was still sleeping, so that I'd have time to take a shower and clean up before he got up. I would never want him to see me sweaty or sloppily dressed. I don't think that cooking should be hidden, but it should be done early in the morning or on Sundays, mostly while the husband is still in bed. The table should be set by the time he has gotten up, so that everything is ready when he appears for breakfast. The husband ought to help with lunch and the children. He can scrub the potatoes and the children can do the dishes while the wife makes sure that everything is in order.

As far as cooking is concerned, many men are good at it; it's not particularly physically oppressive—it can be a lot of fun.

How about washing the dishes and cleaning up?

I think the husband ought to help with that. He really should do the shopping, since it's hard and a heavy job. Planning the shopping, though, is entirely the woman's job, even if the husband is capable of buying a liter of milk or a kilo of meat. But since men hate to stand in line, shopping often gets delegated to women as well.

Are there other things in the home that only a woman can do?

Yes, washing. But the husband should wash his socks and his underwear himself. He ought to, but since no man would dream of it, it becomes the woman's job. Of course a man can clean, but that's also a woman's job. If a man is decent, he'll beat the rugs and take out the garbage.

Is the situation the same when both work full time?

Of course. At home a woman usually does everything. When the husband comes home he reads his paper and watches TV, contrary to what the newspapers say. They show men on March 8* cooking and cleaning and shopping and scrubbing floors. But it's really the women who do everything.

There's a certain difference between working-class families and the intelligentsia. Maybe the intelligentsia have made more progress, but in working-class families it's the way I've described it.

---

* March 8 is International Women's Day. In the Soviet Union, this is nothing but a kind of "ladies' day off" where the men wait on their wives and women co-workers and give them flowers, chocolate, and perfume. Sometimes they also take care of the cooking and the dishes.

How do you think this could be changed?

Things certainly could be made easier; the question is how. For example, in one factory people were given a chance to order food in advance, but when it was time to pick it up they still had to stand in line with several hundred others, so that was no solution. And I don't think psychological change is possible either. Men have become accustomed to thinking that everything at home is woman's work, and it's impossible to change that attitude.

How do you feel about the future?

Actually, I think less and less about the future. It seems meaningless to dream if there's no chance of fulfillment. But of course it's impossible to live without dreams. I dream of giving my son the very best. There's a lot I can't give him, but I'll try anyway. I don't want him to suffer from being defenseless; I want him to be healthy and vigorous and to know everything he wants to know.

It's hard to talk about my wishes for myself. There have been so many that have never been realized. There's a great deal of difference between what I want and reality. I'd like to get an apartment, for instance, but I can't. I'd like to have a dog, but that would be impossible with my neighbors. They don't like animals, and even when I bring a male friend home it's unpleasant. I have a lot of friends all over the country who'd like to come and stay with me, but that would only cause trouble. It's the same for everyone who lives in a communal apartment.

I'd also like to have some pretty clothes—a skirt, a pair of pants, a sweater. I envy girls who have stylish clothes, I always think it's unfair that I can't afford something, but I can't. I have to be content with being clean and neat. I don't have any changes of clothing—only what I have on my back. This is the third winter I've worn these shoes. I can't spend 80 rubles for a pair of new boots.

How can I explain the situation to you? I think you have to be passionately involved with life to ignore everything that's inadequate. But I don't have that involvement anymore. I don't think you should look at life through rose-colored glasses—it's all too gray—but you should be able to see clearly enough to see that if you feel dissatisfied in life it's mostly your own fault. Although I've been in the taiga, realized my dreams, looked around and seen some of the world, I'm still not satisfied with my life. If one chooses one thing, one sacrifices something else. When I was in the taiga I wanted to join a theater school and study acting. I had always dreamed of being an actress. But I was the one who prevented it from happening.

To enjoy life one has to stop looking at the darker side, but I can't seem to do that. I don't feel any joy in just being alive.

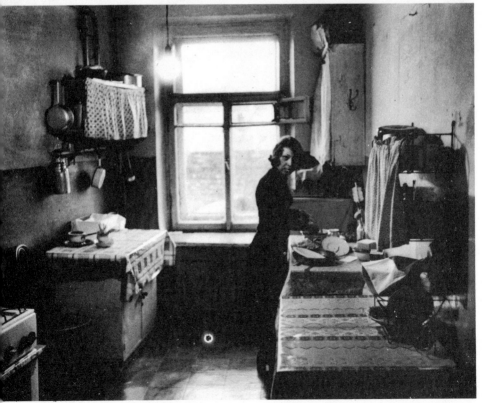

BIRTH CONTROL AND ABORTIONS

The official Soviet community is permeated by sexual puritanism. As a result, the sex education given in Soviet schools is still in the experimental stage. Estonia is the most progressive republic; a course in "personal hygiene" was introduced there in the sixties. Boys and girls are instructed separately. The same is true of the course in problems of intimacy that the Bureau of Marriage Counseling in Leningrad offers to everyone planning to get married. The engaged couple does not attend the same course.

Parents seem unwilling to give their children sexual information. Research has shown that only between 6 and 7 percent of young people learn about sex at home. The most important sources of information are older friends and books.

Information about birth control is also given only sporadically, perhaps because the accessibility of birth-control devices is substandard. Condoms are unreliable and clumsy. The pill isn't always easily available, and possible side effects are seen as a deterrent to its use. In fact, it seems to be a common belief among Soviet women that the mothers of deformed babies in the West had taken the pill.

Diaphragms and intrauterine devices don't seem popular either, partly because of the unpleasantness of going to the gynecologist. "One has to have contacts," many women say, and by that they mean that only then are they well treated and well cared for.

Abortions, which are entirely free during the first three months of pregnancy, are the most commonly used method of birth control. Documentation shows that four out of every five pregnancies end in abortion.

The right to have an abortion has been the subject of discussion for a long time in the Soviet Union. When abortion became legal in 1920, it was not in fact a decisive move toward emancipation but rather an attempt to put a stop to illegal abortions, which were so often fatal.

Even Aleksandra Kollontai* looked at contraception and abortion as bourgeois nonsense and accepted the law concerning free abortion as a necessary evil during the transition period. In 1936, under Stalin, a new and rigorous law concerning the family was introduced, which among other things was designed to raise the birthrate. Although it prohibited abortion, the birthrate remained unchanged, and the number of accidents and deaths from illegal abortions increased. In 1955 abortions again became legal, but they were granted only for medical reasons. Only in 1968 did they again become legal for all women in the Soviet Union.

At the time of this writing, an abortion costs 5 rubles. Even as late as the twelfth week, the operation takes place without drugs. A woman signs in sick for three days but doesn't get any support in the way of advice or consultation. Hospital routines are terribly taxing and consist of endless paperwork

---

* Aleksandra Kollontai (1872–1952) was a Russian revolutionary, commissar, diplomat, and author. In 1923 she was appointed the Soviet Union's minister to Norway—the first woman in the world to hold that diplomatic rank. She was minister to Sweden from 1930 to 1943; ambassador to Sweden from 1943 to 1945.

and questions. Therefore, women who have the money and the proper contacts try to get the abortion performed privately. That way they needn't be absent from work for the three telltale days that a regular abortion requires. Despite the fact that these underground abortions are illegal, they are very common.

Most deliveries take place in hospitals, where sexual prudery follows the woman all the way into the delivery room. To give birth to a child is painful, but above all unaesthetic—or so people think. The most common argument against having the father present at the delivery is that it is too grotesque. At most he is allowed to sit in a room next door. Another reason for his absence is that the woman herself can't always be guaranteed a separate room for delivery; other women in labor may be present as well. Sedatives and anesthetics are rarely given—occasionally laughing gas is used. But courses where prospective mothers can exercise and practice relaxation and baby care do exist.

Mother and child stay in the hospital for a week after the delivery. For the first twenty-four hours the mother is supposed to rest, and she doesn't see the child. The next day, when the baby is brought in to her, it is swaddled so completely that only its head is visible.

N I N A

"I DON'T WANT TO BE CONSIDERED INFERIOR TO MEN."

Nina and her husband, Vova, have their own apartment in
a large building complex about an hour from the center
of Moscow. From the eighth floor there is a view of the
whole area, with twenty or so identical white buildings
surrounding a tremendous excavation. On the narrow streets between
the houses pedestrians are making their way to and from the bus stops
at the great traffic arteries that border the area. Nina thinks a sports
arena is planned for the excavated area, possibly for the Olympics.

Nina and Vova are both twenty-five. They have a little daughter,
Svetka, who will soon be two and a half. Nina works as a data
programmer. In the evenings she studies psychology and pedagogy at
the university. Vova works in the same place and takes the same
courses as Nina at the university.

We visit them on a Saturday, the day when most of the heaviest
household chores have to be done. At the outside door we run into a
young man who is lugging a new sink. He turns out to be Vova.
When we ring their bell Nina is busy with the weekly household
cleaning.

Right away we ask about the apartment, which is unusually large. Yes, they have three rooms, 44 square meters. It's a cooperative apartment, and the money for the down payment came from Nina's parents. The 44 square meters doesn't even include the foyer, which is quite large. Nor is the kitchen or the toilet and bathroom included. They still have hardly any furniture at all, and this contributes to the impression of light and spaciousness. The windows are full of green plants, and in the kitchen dill and parsley are growing on the windowsill.

During the interview little Svetka runs in and out of her room, where the floor is littered with educational toys. Nina, who is very conscious of the importance of the formative years of a child, is eager to talk about how she wants to bring up her daughter. Her conversation is both lively and thoughtful. She is a tall woman, with large gestures and a seemingly endless amount of self-confidence. We ask her to tell us something about her own childhood.

I was born in Moscow. Although in those days the area we lived in was considered to be outside of town, now it's just about in the center. In any case it was beyond the university. I remember when there was nothing there but a big black field and beyond it the enormous illuminated university buildings. That's how it looked when I was a child.

We lived in a wooden house. Both Mama's and Papa's parents were peasants. Papa is an electrician. Both he and Mama work in the same center now, one that dispatches trucks. I also have two younger sisters.

It was fun living in that house. We had a wonderful garden with lots of fruit trees. And I was part of a whole gang of kids who played together. They were mostly boys. We built huts and played all different kinds of ball games.

As a child I had terribly lofty but also terribly vague dreams for my future. Actually, I knew almost nothing about the possibilities that existed. In school we seemed to be isolated from real life. At most we were allowed to make a study visit to some factory, but we never got to participate in any real work. Now a greater effort is made to give students more job orientation in school. There are more study visits, for example, and people from the outside are invited into the school. But in my case it happened quite by chance. I liked math and enrolled in a course at the university. But I gave that up and instead began at a technicum*—partly because the course of study was shorter and I wanted to support myself as soon as possible, since Mama and Papa were having a hard time. But before I started I didn't even know there was such a thing as a technicum. Nor did I know that data processors even existed! It's possible that my friends knew all about it, but my parents weren't well educated, and it may have been the ambience at home that inhibited me a bit. It was my godfather who suggested that I investigate this particular course of study. It seemed like a good idea. But I chose my later studies myself; by then I was much more aware and conscious.

Now I both work and study. I work the regular forty hours a week and study at night. Since my husband takes the same courses, we take turns going to the lectures. That's permitted when one has children. Naturally, our progress is slower than that of students who don't work. For us it will take six years instead of five to finish the basic degree at the university. It's hard, but it's possible to do some studying at our jobs.

We want to manage by ourselves and not be dependent on our parents. Of course we could get a student grant instead of working, but that's never as much as a salary. I make 130 rubles a month and Vova 140. I also don't want to be as isolated from everything as students are. I want to confront our problems, so to speak. Besides, I already have professional training as a computer programmer. These are all the reasons why I don't want to give up working, even though I'm still studying.

Sometimes, of course, we have problems with Svetka. During the day she's at the nursery, but she gets sick often and has to stay at home. Fortunately they're decent on the job and sometimes let us take work home. They don't care whether I work afternoons or evenings instead of mornings. My working

---

* A technicum is a kind of technical high school specializing in vocational training.

time is quite flexible. That isn't the case at factories, where the working hours are strictly controlled.

In the morning Vova's almost always the one who takes Svetka to the nursery. She's going through a phase where she cries when we leave her; that's very hard on me. They leave at about seven-thirty and I sleep until eight. Then Vova and I have breakfast, and between nine and half past we leave for work, which takes about fifty minutes with bus and subway.

Except for taking Svetka to school we haven't divided up the household chores very strictly. The one who happens to be free when the stores are least crowded does the shopping. But I would guess I do a bit more than Vova, although he claims that everything is equally divided. That's more or less true. He washes, cleans, does the dishes. But I still feel that somehow I have to hold everything together.

We quit work around six; sometimes a little earlier, sometimes a little later. If both of us have to go to a lecture my mother comes and takes care of Svetka. We usually have two lectures a night, from six-thirty until nine-thirty. We get home about ten-thirty, have tea, talk until midnight, or perhaps until one or two in the morning.

Most things about marriage are fine. I'm glad that we share things equitably. Vova cares a lot about our child, much more now than before. If you had met me a while ago, I would have said that I wasn't very happy. He didn't think it was important to pay so much attention to her; children have always managed without too much fussing, he claimed.

Now I'm more bothered by the fact that it's so hard to keep order around here. That's because we haven't bought any furniture yet. It becomes very important for everyone to remember to pick up after themselves, and Vova is even less ambitious than I am in this area.

I don't think that sex is the most important part of our marriage. We do have some problems, but that's probably because we got married quite recently, and also because we're working so hard. We worry about our jobs, our studies, and we have our hands full when we come home. And then, sometimes, you just don't feel like it at all. When one has had a chance to rest, it all comes back.

It's very important for me to be able to talk to Vova about my personal ambitions. But I notice that he doesn't have an equally great need for this. He wants to work on his own projects and gets bored with all my plans and my talk. And he detests going to the country, which I love! Those are our problems, but they aren't that great. And things will probably get better as time goes on if we work on overcoming them.

I really don't have any free time at all. There's so much to do and not enough time to do it in. Basically, I look on my studies as a hobby. After work I devote myself to my hobby. So you could say that I spend my leisure time reading. But I also love being in the woods, and if I had more free time I'd buy a bicycle!

I'd also take Svetka swimming and read novels, which I don't have time to do now. Play the guitar. Study languages. See my friends. Travel. Sew and knit. I wouldn't have a free minute!

Is it a uniquely feminine problem not to have any free time? I don't know. Is the household a woman's responsibility? We all wish that household chores would take much less time, that there were well-stocked stores in the vicinity, and that services —places for washing and things like that—would be on the premises. We would also like to have more nurseries and day-care centers and have them function better so that there isn't such a tremendous difference between the needs of parents and what actually exists. One solution would be for several families to band together—that happens in other countries, I know. But here the housing problem gets in the way. We have friends with whom we could share baby-sitting, but they live on the other side of Moscow, and it would be next to impossible for us to arrange to live close to each other. If we could arrange it, life would certainly be easier. We have the same ideas about how to bring up children, and Svetka wouldn't have to go to a nursery.

As for women's problems . . . I don't really know whether they exist as such. What I've been talking about concerns both women and men, and basically it's the government's problem.

However, it's true that most women limit themselves to their family. I mean, for them the job plays a secondary role.

Equality doesn't only mean equal rights. It should consist of both rights and obligations. That also includes sex. If a man can have a lover, a woman should have the same right. Both ought to have the same right to travel and the same right to leisure time, the right to devote themselves to their personal interests and not only stand by the stove. Obligations vis-à-vis the children and the housework and toward each other should be shared.

I myself feel a strong desire always to be just as good as men —I don't want to be inferior in strength and endurance. Perhaps I can't be quite as good as men, but in any case I can be better than other women. If I'm part of a ski competition, it's the men I compete against, not the women. If we go hiking in the mountains I want to have a heavier backpack than the other girls, and I usually manage to run. I'm the same when it comes to my work.

I keep on coming back to the fact that rights and obligations should be divided equally. Perhaps I stress obligations because some people seem to think that women are more or less empty-headed. And yet women are very often more intelligent than men! I see many instances of this where I work. So occasionally situations arise where I feel that I have to prove that I'm just as good as a man. But most of the time I don't feel that I'm *in opposition* to men. Do you understand? I don't like to fight if I can avoid it. I like to work together with men, but I *don't* like to feel as if I'm in a subordinate position. I don't like it when they come to a mutual decision and then deign to inform me of it only after it's already been made.

No, I get involved. I have my own opinions. And I'm capable, too.

This is what I think a woman should be like. I got it from a film I recently saw: "Party woman, sportswoman, community woman, and beautiful woman." Something like that. I like people who are involved. A woman ought to have a well-rounded education and be intellectually inclined. Interested in everything and eager to learn. And she has to be a good mother!

Femininity to me is synonymous with gentleness. I used to be exactly like a boy, and now when sometimes I really want to be feminine I don't always succeed. I really prefer to be the sporty type, and I'd like to make more of a mark in sports. Recently I started scuba diving, but I had to stop for lack of time.

In certain situations femininity is important. At work and in important discussions it isn't vital. Putting up a good fight can be more effective. But during free time and when relaxing with other people it's important that a woman be gracious, both for herself and for others.

I like to be considered feminine, but I want to be appreciated for my intellect. I think I'm far from dumb. And I want people to see that I'm independent.

I also want to try to have good relationships with children. I'd like to at least succeed at being a good mother.

I'm going to have at least three children. Then we'll see. I have one now, and when I have the second I'll know better how many I can manage. But at least three, I hope. I'm trying to plan now when it would be best to have the second. I don't think having several children would affect my career—it would affect my leisure time and my studies instead. But that's a question of planning, and of bringing up the children so that they understand that "Mama's studying, so don't interrupt her." I've already started with that. Children should also be taught that when Mama is working, they have to help. When they've finished we can play together. Both independence and responsibility must exist within a family—and freedom.

If Vova and I can't get our degrees at the same time, we have to do it in turn. One needs about two years to write a dissertation. That's the basis of one's career.

I'd like to take part in changing the whole educational system, including professional training. Children's characters should be developed at a much earlier age. You see, I feel positive about communism, and I'd even dare to say that in questions of education I know what needs to be done. Until the educational system is radically changed—although of course they're working on it—I feel that I have something to contribute. To be part of shaping the Communist human being is what I want to do most of all.

As I see it, the grounds of morality are laid during childhood. During the early years it's through fairy tales and the example of adults that a child's moral fiber is first established. Then comes the association with peers, and gradually the association with fellow workers.

They tell an anecdote about Makarenko:* A mother asks him, "When should one start educating a child?" "How old is your child?" "Two weeks old." "Madam, you're already two weeks too late!"

Children have to go to day-care centers, of course. But to tell the truth, I'd rather keep them at home—probably because I've studied psychology, which has made me more conscious and demanding.

You see, often the day-care personnel here are not trained well for their work. And, of course, all children are different. In a day-care center they can't focus on one child. Because they have so many, there are lots of rules to follow. And the staff is so varied that the education the children receive is uneven. Education is often an unconscious process, so the kids get a lot of different messages. On the other hand, there's *something* that they all get in common; otherwise we couldn't talk about "the Soviet citizen."

* The ideas of Anton Makarenko (1888–1939) completely dominated Soviet pedagogy until the end of the 1950s. The theories of collective child rearing that he developed in connection with the rehabilitation of youth criminals in the twenties and thirties are still the basis for education in Soviet day-care centers and schools in general.

Here no men work in nurseries or day-care centers. Perhaps it wouldn't be a bad idea if they did. But all women, no matter how different, have something in common—an inherent goodness, a common tenderness, maternal feeling, a concern about the future. This nurturing is more a part of women than it is of men. If a man were asked what he is going to do with his future, he would describe his plans. But a woman would answer, "I am going to care for my children."

ONE CHILD OR SEVERAL?

In 1950, 26.7 children were born to every 1,000 inhabitants in the Soviet Union. In 1974 the number was down to 18.* The birthrate is lowest in the European areas of the Soviet Union.

Authorities have long been worried over the shrinking birthrate. The prohibition against abortion enacted in 1936 and the more stringent laws governing divorce enacted in 1944 were a dramatic effort to strengthen the Soviet family. It was also in 1944 that the government began to give medals to women who had given birth to and brought up a large number of children. A woman who has given birth to ten children still has the title Heroic Mother, and those who have had seven to nine children receive a Medal of Honor. The Motherhood Medal, made of bronze and silver, goes to women who have had five or six children. But most Soviet women feel that economic subsidies, part-time work, better day care, and more extensive community services would contribute more to

* Editor's note: In 1981 in the United States, 15.9 children were born to every 1,000 inhabitants.

bringing about a higher birthrate than a lot of newspaper articles about Heroic Mothers and their families.

Thus far, the state supports families in the following ways: Women have the right to 56 days of maternity leave before delivery and 56 days of leave after delivery, both with full salary. They also have the right to stay at home without pay for a year after the child's birth without losing their jobs, but most women can't afford to stay at home that long without an income. Some women don't want to stay home for a year and try to locate some kind of part-time work, which is almost impossible to find.

When the third child is born, women get a bonus of 20 rubles. The fourth baby brings 65 rubles and child support of 4 rubles per month until the child is five. Otherwise, only unwed mothers get child support for the first child. They can collect it until the child is thirteen. Women with a lot of children have another advantage—the right to collect a pension at the age of fifty.

Most families are dependent on the woman's contribution to their income. But when the impossible is demanded of her— that she manage to work outside the home as well as take care of the family without her husband's help—she will refuse to have more than one child, even if this decision goes against her own desires.

ELENA
STEPANOVNA
AND
ALEVTINA
GIORGIEVNA

**"DURING THE WAR WOMEN'S LIVES BECAME
TERRIBLY DIFFICULT."**

E*lena Stepanovna is in her seventies. She receives a pension
from her former position as a librarian and from time to time
publishes an article. She complains that she isn't able to write
much because she has to care for her grandchild. He goes to
school, of course, but she's responsible for him—she has to get him
ready and be there when he comes home.*

*Elena Stepanovna doesn't want to talk about her life or answer
personal questions. Instead we ask her to tell us how the woman's
role has changed during her lifetime.*

I don't consider the Soviet woman to be terribly different from
women anywhere else. It's hard to imagine otherwise. What's
more likely is that a woman's particular physical and psychological characteristics are greater and more important than the
ways in which society has tried to mold her and teach her.

But perhaps our women are more determined, more active, bolder, and have more initiative because those characteristics are developed in the work place. I'm not really sure. When you get down to it, a woman is always a woman. Her maternal instincts are a determining factor.

When I was a young girl after the Revolution, I vividly remember how women in my immediate circle—the big-city intelligentsia—enthusiastically accepted the world that was opening up. We could participate in everything that was happening. We felt completely equal to men—in every-thing!

Coeducation was established when I was a child; I always studied with boys. My school was good; there was a real feel-ing of camaraderie among us. Maybe it was the quality of the education, the inspiring teachers, that contributed to our feeling that men and women were equal, not only from a legal point of view but also where possibilities in life were concerned—in other words, in capacity and talent. Yes, I think that the at-mosphere in which I grew up *developed* our potential as much as the boys'. We all concentrated on our studies and on further-ing our education. We were interested in everything, fascinated by everything.

Then the situation for women changed. Suddenly women got heavier burdens to bear as a result of everything that was happening in our country. There was the war, and women's lives became terribly difficult.

In a way, women became stronger through their hardships, but in another way they were destroyed. Women were forced to engage in work that was way beyond their strength. Of course this injured these women, perhaps the whole postwar generation.

What was most damaged was women's innermost being. After the war there were so terribly many widows here who were forced to shoulder the responsibility of bringing up their children alone.

Of course, women got a lot out of their enforced indepen-dence because they were alone to make important decisions.

But they became more masculine, more decisive, even more like men psychologically.

When I was very young, laws were instituted that simplified relationships in sexual matters. In a way, they became *too* simple. A couple could get married on Thursday, and on Saturday one of the spouses could go to ZAGS* and get a divorce—even without the partner's knowledge. It was probably the very first expression of what freedom, complete freedom, ought to be. Then came the terrible period when abortions were forbidden. Imagine the woman's plight when she had to work, already had two children, and discovered that she was expecting a third, a fourth, a fifth. . . . How was it possible to deny her an abortion? It was a dreadful time, a brutal time. I myself saw some of the awful results of those policies. There were so many women who could never become mothers because at a certain time in their lives they had been forced to get "nonmedical" assistance in aborting a fetus. Many died. Now that we have free abortions, a woman can decide for herself whether or not she wants to give birth, and that's only for the better.

What we need today is better information about sex. Young people ought to be more prepared when they enter into marriage. There's an abysmal ignorance regarding sexual matters, and very little literature. Recently they've begun talking about information centers—we need more trained personnel, sexologists, psychologists. But you have to realize that it would be hard for everyone to get this information. These centers would have to be available in every residential neighborhood in the cities! Another possibility would be to distribute books, books that everyone could buy and read. This is an area in which we have to do something radical and fast!

So far we haven't paid much attention to the double load a woman carries. Of course, general services have to improve. We ought to be able to do our shopping much more quickly, without wasting so much time. I'm sure that every housewife

* Civilian registration bureaus; the everyday name for the Soviet "marriage palaces."

would be able to tell you how to improve the way food and other products are distributed. In the press they're also beginning to talk about "flex time," or flexible work hours, which would help women enormously.

Then there's talk about extending maternity leave. Right now it's four months with pay and the right to a year's leave without pay. But there are so many who can't afford to take that amount of time. Just think of all the single mothers! And they aren't the only ones who have to work although they have a newborn baby! So a longer paid maternity leave is needed. At least it should be possible to get a certain percentage of one's salary for a longer period, if not the whole salary. In fact, better organization is needed in every area. For example, why should a woman turn up at her place of work every day when she could do the work at home? Office work, for instance. She could do most of the work at home and perhaps go to the office once a week. If one asked women about these problems and listened seriously to their answers, I think some of them could be resolved.

A few days later we are invited to have tea with Elena Stepanovna. She has just spent several hours traveling across Moscow to fetch her friend, Alevtina Giorgievna. "I wanted you to meet the marvelous Alevtina Giorgievna," she says, and proceeds to introduce her friend. "Alevtina Giorgievna and I have only known each other for a couple of years, but we've become fast friends. Alevtina Giorgievna was born in the Orlov district, in the country. She has lived in Moscow for a couple of years. She has had a very hard and difficult life, but she has been able to sustain a wonderful lightness of spirit, innate goodness, and inner calm. This is what I admire so much in her. And I'd like you to hear her tell about her life."

Alevtina Giorgievna immediately begins to talk. Her voice is light and plaintive. One gets the feeling that during her long life this voice has had to express worry and grief, pain and compassion.

Papa died in 1908 when I was only a year old. There were three of us—two girls and a boy. Mother came from a large family

—they numbered twenty-two with all the sisters-in-law and the children. Then the family split up. Mama was given a samovar and a horse. Those were her possessions when she began to live on her own, plus a plot of arable land and a small piece of woodland. I was eight at the time, and I remember it well. We began to cut down trees to build a house. My sister and brother had to go off to other villages to work for wealthy people. My brother was thirteen at the time, I remember. I had to go with my mother to work for a family of landed gentry. The lady was very nice.

When spring came we had made a little money and could build our house. So at least then we had a home, although my brother and sister had to serve at other people's houses all the time until they got married. I got married to a boy from the village when I was seventeen. He was tall and handsome and he liked to sing. At that time I had had four years of school, and that was all I ever got.

When the war came we all moved in together: my sister, who was a widow with three children; I with my three; and my sister-in-law, who had five. My husband and my brother of course were off fighting the war. The Germans came and forced us to work for them. We had to build bunkers where they could stable their horses. During that winter my sister-in-law died of exhaustion, leaving five children. I took care of them.

We were evacuated for three years, but the whole time we lived quite close to our village, which was right at the front. Toward the end of the war there were terrible struggles all around us. We hid in our miserable mud huts, which were our only shelter. Finally, our own soldiers came and helped us to get behind the front. We walked and walked until we got to a sovkhoz* where we stayed for about a week. My husband had been killed and was buried in a mass grave right there. He had been recruited immediately at the outset of the war. He was wounded and died in a hospital in 1942.

* A sovkhoz is a Soviet state-owned farm that pays wages to its workers.

After a couple of weeks we returned to our village. It had been completely destroyed, and there were bodies all over the place. The air was almost impossible to breathe. We tried to find places to sleep, and used grass as blankets. But we were almost devoured by flies. I remember how I tried to console my little Tonya, who was five. I caressed her and caressed her; that was all I could do for her. But we survived. Later, soldiers came and helped us bury all the dead. And we began to try to live there; a wall went up here and there. All that was left of our two brick houses were two corners, and we tried to build from there.

It was only women and children who had returned. All the men had been taken by the war. Then a man came from the city to help us organize the work. We had to name a woman as chairwoman of the kolkhoz, and women as "brigadiers," and so on.

I was chosen as chairwoman. We worked around the clock. The war was hard on us.

When spring came we had to walk to get seed—sixty kilometers back and forth—and we had to carry sixteen kilos each. It was early spring; we had tied rags around our feet and were wet the whole time. We carried the seed home, but all the fields were ruined because they had made trenches there. So the women had to till them up again. Look at my fingers; they're ruined from that work! They don't hurt, but it's not nice to have fingers like that. And then we had to plow, and we had to use spades. I traveled to several other kolkhozy where they had horses; we didn't even have a cow. Everything was gone. Finally we managed to get three horses and plows, and later we got a tractor, too.

But there were mines everywhere. And so many children blown into bits! One woman lost both her little boys at the same time. There were still mines around, you know, although the war was so long ago, but the front was right there, so one can imagine how much debris was left.

For three years I was leader of the kolkhoz. It was very difficult. Now it would be much easier. Now it's only a question of leadership in work, because all the necessary supplies are available—machines, everything. But at that time! If you know how many difficult days I spent!

When my oldest boy graduated from eighth grade I was very worried about how to plan for him. A cousin suggested that I try to get him into the railroad training program. We brought along some bread and potatoes to eat and walked the sixty kilometers because I didn't have the fare. The boy was tall and skinny and not very strong. He was ashamed because he didn't have decent pants. I told him not to be embarrassed because we were so poor, but that if he was sensible and started school we would be able to get him a pair of pants soon enough.

When we got to the school we had to show his diploma. Then they looked at the boy, and he was such a pathetic sight. They told me I had to outfit him better. "But I have nothing to outfit him with," I said. "Why don't you take him and teach him and outfit him here?" I said. And they accepted him, but it took a long time before he got any clothes. I sent him pants as fast as I could once I had gotten some insurance money from my husband's death.

One time he came home. It was terribly cold. He had walked all the way and tied his shoes together with wire. He had come because he had worn out his shoes too soon and had to have new ones. "All right, all right," I said to calm him, and gave him something to eat. It was around midnight. So I made a bed for him on top of the stove. In the morning I went and stood at the front door and wondered what to do. "Good Lord, what am I going to do? How can I get him shoes so he can go back to town and won't have to stay here on the kolkhoz? Good Lord," I said, and crossed myself. "Help me." And then I thought that I would go to the shoemaker to ask him to make the boy a pair of shoes. He asked me if we didn't have any old shoes around, and actually we did have a whole bag of old shoes that we had collected when we came back to the village. They were from the dead soldiers.

"Go and get the bag and I'll make the boy a pair of shoes," the shoemaker said. But I had no money to pay him with, so I had to go to the teacher and ask her for some. And she gave it to me. So I got him off to school again. Later on they gave him a fine uniform and he looked so handsome! My other boy also got away from the kolkhoz. We got him into another school in town and then he went into the army.

But then when Tonya finished school it was the same thing all over again. Where would I send her? How would I get her away from the kolkhoz? Finally my sister-in-law in Moscow offered to take her. I didn't have anything to give her—no money, no clothes. I made her a skirt and a blouse out of material that had been given to a relative when she had a baby. And then I took her to Moscow. But she was only fourteen, and no trade school would accept her until she was sixteen. So for two years she worked in a basement sorting goods. My lovely Tonya! When she turned sixteen she came home to get her pass,* but they didn't want to give her one. They wanted her to stay and work in the kolkhoz office.

"I'll never let that happen," I said. And after a lot of haggling I got them to give her a pass and sent her off to school in the city.

Alevtina Giorgievna goes on to tell us more about her daughter, about how she got married and about her present work.

What changes have been the most important in women's lives here?

A lot has changed! I don't quite know how to say it, but before, women were so much better. They were conscientious and

---

* Pass or passport. From the age of sixteen on, Soviet citizens are required to carry a national registration card that they have to produce in a multitude of situations— such as when seeking employment, registering at a hotel, etc. As recently as 1975 the government resisted issuing domestic passports to the kolkhoz peasants, which practically forced them to stay on their kolkhozy whether they wanted to or not. This is the reason for Alevtina Giorgievna's efforts to get her children away from the kolkhoz and into the towns, where they could get professional training. From 1976 on, passports have been issued to kolkhoz peasants. It is believed that by now everyone has received his or her passport.

weren't so forward. Now they're rude and show no respect for older people.

But aren't women much better off materially today?

Of course! Dear me, the way we looked after the war! We had no clothes—only rags. The kolkhoz was so poor, and still everything had to go to the state. We couldn't buy a thing then, but now everyone is so well off!

My Tonya, for example, is just an ordinary worker, but she has everything she needs. Except she has only one child, and I keep on telling her she ought to get herself another one. "Just think if something should happen," I say. "You'll regret it for the rest of your life!"

But that's the way it is. Women have to work a certain number of years to get their pension benefits. If a woman stays home when she's young then she has to work longer when she's old. If you don't put in your years you won't get your pension. So people are forced to work.

But tell me, my dear, is it good for a child when its mother isn't at home? You can't leave a small child alone at home, and so most women do stay home for a while. There's no nursery in our kolkhoz because there are so few children born nowadays. Women don't want to have any. It's very bad. Everyone ought to have two or three at least. But people don't want to have children.

PENSIONS

The retirement age in the Soviet Union is relatively low: fifty-five for women and sixty for men. To receive a full pension women must have worked twenty years, men twenty-five.

Pensions come from the government, which means that there are no deductions from salaries for this purpose. The pension is calculated from a percentage of the salary and is inversely related to it: The higher the salary, the lower the percentage (although as a rule not lower than 50 to 55 percent), and the lower the salary, the higher the percentage (the minimum salary merits 100 percent). The pensions are tax-free and are paid by the month.

When individuals retire, it doesn't mean that they are no longer allowed to work. Everyone can continue working and receive their full or partial pension besides.

But the truth behind these facts can be rather grim. The actual average pension is very low—about 40 rubles a month; the minimum income required for subsistence has been calculated at 50 rubles. Many older people receive a certain amount of security from the fact that they live with their grown children. But people who have reached retirement age are actually being encouraged to continue working, and the fact that as many as 25 percent do so—often in badly paid jobs such as cleaning women, watchmen, or elevator operators—suggests that people need to supplement their pension payments.

L Y U B A

"INEQUITIES DON'T ALWAYS GIVE RISE TO ANGER."

L*yuba lives in a house about to be torn down. Unrenovated since the war, it has been condemned. During its final stage it will function as a workers' barracks.*

Lyuba and her family have gotten a new apartment in a high rise. From a wooden house in the center of town to a concrete suburb: Does she really want that? It seems so. When we look at the old wooden house we agree that its charm is limited. Of course there's no bathroom; clothes have to be washed in the windowless kitchen and baths taken there as well. The toilet is an outhouse in the yard.

We are introduced to Lyuba's husband, Vitya, and her boy, Alyosha. Lyuba tells us that Vitya has been sick almost all of his life and that it is she who more or less has brought him back to life. Now she is supporting the family while Vitya is finally going to learn a profession.

Lyuba sits on the double bed as she talks. There is a shelf with a collection of stones, some drawings on the walls, two chairs, some branches in a vase. That's all, but the room is overcrowded. The window is open, and birds twitter during the interview. Lyuba's voice is also as light as a bird's, which doesn't quite fit in with her robust frame. She has pale, slightly slanted eyes and curly reddish-brown hair with bangs. Her clothes seem soft and comfortable—a sweater and wide-ribbed corduroy pants. She has strong hands with short nails, stained with nicotine. It's clear that life hasn't always treated her gently.

I'm an artist, thirty-two years old. I was married once before and have a son from that marriage. I was twenty-one when we got married, and I already had the baby. We were divorced when I was twenty-five. Now I'm married for the second time —six months ago.

A lot of people get divorced very early here. Why do you think that's so?

We know so little about life when we marry; we become independent so late. Almost without exception young people are dependent on their parents to help out economically. The money problem becomes especially acute if a couple has a child and the woman has to stop working. Here a family can't possibly live on one salary. Never! Well, perhaps two people can live on the man's salary, but with a child it's impossible. And it almost never happens that a young person can have her own apartment which she can take care of herself. Newly married couples have to wait a long time to get their own apartment and have to live with their parents in the meantime. If the parents have means, they can buy into a cooperative and the young people can move in after a year or two. But sometimes they have to live with their parents for ten years, or perhaps all their lives.

Very often young people divorce just after they've moved away from their parents. Before they moved they were still like children, and only when they start living by themselves do they notice that they're very different from each other and that they can't live together. Or if the parents don't like their daughter-in-law or son-in-law, there always seems to be a way of making the children divorce. There are quarrels and . . . well, it can be just awful.

So I think that one of the main reasons people divorce is that young people never learn to take charge of their own lives but are always beholden to their parents—completely bound, both economically and morally.

What was it like in your case?

I got married—out of stupidity! At home the atmosphere was so cold and unpleasant that as soon as a boy treated me like a human being I decided that this was love, and love for life. When we began to live together we discovered that it didn't work so well. But my husband had just been assigned to work in Kalinin for three years* and we were able to live by ourselves. And we already had the boy, so I found a way of getting used to it and even enjoying it.

He served his three years and we moved back to Moscow and lived with my parents. But he stayed away from home more and more and finally didn't come home at all. The atmosphere was very bad. With him there were five of us in the apartment. But since he was registered with his parents, and only the four of us were registered in our apartment, we couldn't get a large one because we had more than five square meters per person. There was nothing I could do. My parents didn't want to try to change apartments, and to live together with them was impossible, so we got divorced.

What did your first husband do?

He was also an artist. We met at the Academy of Art. He was three years ahead of me, and when he finished I had to give up my studies and go with him to Kalinin. After five years I began to study again, but he was against that; he probably felt I was

---

* A three-year contract. After graduating, students are usually assigned a place to work for three years before they are allowed to seek employment on their own.

more gifted than he. When I started to do well, he got jealous and said that a woman should stay at home and take care of the house.

What did you do during that time in Kalinin?

I stayed at home with the boy. I tried to send him to a day-care center, but he became ill. They so often do in day-care centers. If a mother has a job she may end up staying home almost half the time when the child is sick—at least during the first three years. It's so common for children to be sick that employers actually try to avoid hiring women with small children. But of course that's not acknowledged officially. Women with small children can still get jobs, but employers avoid hiring them for more responsible positions.

So I stayed at home. Sometimes I got away and went to the factory where my husband worked and made some jewelry. A lot of people make this kind of jewelry in Moscow now, but I think I was the first!

How did you get this apartment?

It belongs to my in-laws. They lived here together with my present husband, his sister and brother-in-law, and their boy. Actually the sister and brother-in-law had a two-room apartment already, but when they got married they took this one instead, and the in-laws very soon got another one-room apartment right in this neighborhood. My father-in-law was wounded in the war and had priority. Then they managed to buy a one-bedroom apartment for their daughter, and this was left to us.

We have three rooms, but one is locked. My sister-in-law and her husband are a bit difficult, a bit unpleasant. To be clever, they got divorced before she got her co-op, so the co-op became hers and her son's, while the husband supposedly stayed in that locked room. That means that the room still is theirs, and when this house is torn down they'll have the right to another room and will perhaps be able to get a larger apartment. Or perhaps they're thinking of selling the room. In any case, they're going to make use of the room in some way, and of course it's understandable, since the cooperative was terribly expensive. I don't know exactly, but I think the down payment was at least 5,000 rubles, and besides that, they have to make monthly payments for at least twenty years.

I don't say anything . . . everyone arranges his life the best he can. I myself wouldn't go to that much trouble . . . but it's their business. Many people here enter into bogus marriages and divorces. There are supposedly two thousand marriages like that here, because it's also a way to become a registered inhabitant of Moscow.

So we've got the apartment—without paying a thing! But now that the house is coming down we're moving to the suburbs. I went out to see the building; it has twelve floors with five entrances. There are two- and three-room apartments. All the two-room apartments face south, so even if we had gotten three rooms we might have chosen the two-room one because of the sun. It's on the tenth floor. Not big, but it has a bathroom, an electric stove, linoleum on the floors. The ceilings are quite low . . . but it's going to be all right. After all, we don't have to share it!

What does your husband do?

He has been sick a lot and was unable to do his military service —and he didn't study, so although he's twenty-eight, he has no education at all. He's had a lot of different jobs, and that doesn't look good on his record. He was advised to take a job and to stick to it for at least a year. Right now he's a superintendent; he'll complete his year in April. I'm going to manage the family somehow until he gets some professional training. He's trying to make up his mind what to do. His present job is terrible. You want to know what he makes? Only 67 rubles a month.

Can you manage without your parents' help?

No. I make some money selling my ceramic things, but without his parents we wouldn't be able to buy a single piece of furniture for the new apartment. We don't even have a bed. His parents gave us 500 rubles for furniture, and still give us 30 to 40 rubles a month—sometimes 60 rubles. Of course I would have managed somehow, worked as a cleaning woman . . . but instead I've been able to spend a year learning how to draw and sculpt again, after three years of being out of touch—and that was all thanks to his parents. They're fine people, and I'm very grateful.

Were you born in Moscow?

No, I grew up in a town forty kilometers away. There's an airport out there; you live with airplanes over your head all the time. Papa was a foreman, the manager of repairs at the local railroad buildings. Mama was a librarian at a local resort. I was the only child.

Our family relationship wasn't too good. Mama said that she only stayed with Papa for appearance's sake—and for mine. They fought a lot. Papa was often drunk; all construction workers drink. In order to do a good job they have to get tanked up—or so they say. If a foreman receives a bottle he does his best. If you don't give him anything he does nothing. Papa was always drinking on the job as well as at home, and Mama was always at him. Somehow they didn't seem to notice me.

From the age of fourteen, fifteen, I dreamed of getting away from home. I thought I'd get through high school, get myself a good job, pay back Mama for all she had done to educate me, and then have nothing to do with her.

It actually happened that way. Although I haven't given her any money. But . . . I avoid having anything to do with her.

We have different points of view. She thinks she's so much better than anyone else, and demands eternal gratitude for anything she has done. She always thinks first and foremost of herself. I think one should never give up one's essential self for someone else, but she demands obedience in absolutely everything.

What was school like?

Nothing special. Anyone with normal intelligence or a little above doesn't have to do a thing. Nobody does homework, everyone copies from the books before classes begin. There's no education in morality either. The classes are too large. The teachers aren't interested in students as human beings. If the students do what they're told, then the teachers are content. The Young Pioneer Organization* and Komsomol don't play the slightest role in the life of the students. But everyone has to belong to the Komsomol—otherwise you can't get into the university. There are unpleasant repercussions for those who aren't members.

Once at a meeting we were caught up by youthful enthusiasm and asked questions such as "What should a Komsomol member be and do?" and so on. It was a meeting without an adult leader, and when we later gave an account of the discussion, we were told to leave subjects like that alone in the future.

Already as a child I could see the difference between ideals and reality. I felt it even though I couldn't express it. But when I was around fifteen I went to a youth leader whom I admired very much and asked him why it is that people say and write one thing and then do another. He replied that it was growing pains, that we were underdeveloped on a cultural level. For a while I accepted that, but now I feel that there wasn't much truth in what he said—except that, God knows, the cultural level is very low!

* The Young Pioneer Organization is the Soviet Communist Party's youth organization for children between the ages of seven and fifteen. Practically all children are members.

What made you decide to become an artist?

I've always enjoyed drawing and working with my hands. In the fourth grade I began doing ceramics under the guidance of an excellent teacher who was a sculptress. She was as serious about her work as she was about her students.

Later, when I finished school, I didn't know what to do at all. I didn't know anything, hadn't seen anything. I'd visited a Young Pioneer camp once; otherwise I had spent all my summer holidays with my grandmother, a hundred kilometers from Moscow. And once I'd been to the Black Sea with my parents. For a child it was boring. I got tired of looking at the sea and collecting stones. No, the only thing I knew about was ceramics, so I decided to learn more, and that way I could also study drawing, painting, and sculpture. Mama wanted me to become a doctor. But that very fact made me lose interest in the profession. I wanted to choose myself. But you know what I liked best in school? Drivers' education—I was crazy about it, I was the best in my class! But since my childhood, Mama had imbued me with the idea that someone who didn't have a profession was just shit. It was typical of her generation to rate people like that. I knew I wanted to work with my hands, but the importance of higher education was so drummed into me that I never once considered if it was right or wrong. I chose to work at an art career, which combines intellectual and practical work. And I'm glad I did it—I like the work.

After school I worked for a year, then I went to school for three years at the Art Institute. I was behind my peers, and it was hard to catch up with them. They knew about the Impressionists, for instance, and I'd never heard of them.

I met my first husband at the institute. I thought I was in love. When I became pregnant the doctors actually pleaded with me to have an abortion so that I wouldn't ruin my life. But I didn't want to do like the others: have a relationship, then an abortion, then start a new relationship, and so on . . . so I decided to have the baby. "I'll love it and it will love me, and we'll be happy together," I thought to myself. So I got a job at a factory far away. I didn't tell anyone I was pregnant. During that whole time my boyfriend didn't suggest getting married; he didn't want to. But then he was transferred to the job in Kalinin, felt lonely, said he couldn't live without me. I went with him, and I had the little guy you just saw. We hadn't lived together previously, but when we moved in together I saw that it wouldn't work. But there was the child, and where do you go with a baby? My mother came and saw that I was unhappy. She wanted to help me find a room for myself and the child. But she nagged at me so much not to let people know that my husband and I had had a child before we got married that I decided I'd rather stay with my husband. It wasn't all that bad. We didn't argue; he didn't drink. But there was no closeness or communication. But then, I didn't know you could have that.

Did you have any sex education in school?

None at all. That kind of information comes by word of mouth —through one's girl friends. Even today, my mother acts as if she didn't know how babies are made. When I began to spend time with boys I knew there were such things as condoms, and I had also read about other methods of birth control. But they're not reliable, and the pill is really dangerous. It's difficult, especially at the beginning of a relationship; not everyone can start right in talking about contraceptives. For girls who are shy, the first few times are hard. You don't want to start using the pill right away, and it's not so easy to tell the boy to use condoms. In order to get another kind of contraceptive you have to know a doctor, who will give you something decent. So most women try to get along without, and everything depends on how considerate and sensitive the man is. So many abortions are done; statistics are published on how many are done in hospitals, but then there are also the secret ones. . . .

Secret?

A private abortion costs 35 to 40 rubles. Usually nurses do them. Also doctors. Everyone knows about it, but nobody talks about it.

Why aren't all abortions done in hospitals?

It's taken for granted that if a woman is absent from work for three days she's having an abortion. If she isn't married people start talking; if she is, maybe she doesn't want people to know. Hospital records are public, so women try to avoid going there. Often women come to hospitals after they've tried to induce abortions by taking medicine or by other means and haven't succeeded. By that time the fetus is far along and the hospital staff bawls them out. "Tell us what you took," they say, "otherwise we won't help you." Here everyone is afraid of getting pregnant, terrified of having to have an abortion. It's difficult and painful; I should know, I had one at the hospital. Now they've started to give painkillers. But outside the cities they don't—only some kind of injection that doesn't work. We hoped that things would improve when the pill appeared. I heard the pill mentioned for the first time seven or eight years ago. Yet the first time I was able to buy them was six years ago. Sometimes you can get them, sometimes you can't. Now I haven't seen them for four months. That's the way it is. Sometimes they disappear for months and then turn up again. But now women are afraid of them, too. It's considered safer to have an abortion than to take the pill.

What were conditions like when you had your baby?

My baby was born in a little infirmary in a community outside Kalinin. It was great because I was the only one who had a baby that day. The midwife and her assistant spent all their time with me, talked to me, helped me. I've heard about what it can be like to have a baby here in Moscow, alone, with no one to help. Of course that doesn't happen every day, but it's quite certain that it *does* happen. No, I can't complain; it was good to give birth in a small hospital. If there's a complication, there's always a doctor near who can come right away.

After me a gypsy woman gave birth. She was forty, but already an old woman. It was her tenth child. They had to assist her for three days, and they did. She was completely worn out. She didn't have any milk but I had plenty, so I gave some to her child, too. I think in the country it's more humane. The doctor knows where the patient lives, whether her family has a cow, or grows good tomatoes in their garden.

Did you receive sedatives during your labor pains?

No, and I think that's right, because the mother and child can be damaged by them. I think they give laughing gas in Moscow, but usually it's a natural birth.

After Alyosha was born I heard about natural childbirth. I read that "thanks to the progress made by our doctors, women are able to give birth almost without pain." But I had been totally unprepared.

When I got to the maternity ward and my labor pains began, I got frightened. I screamed so that the poor fathers who had come to look at their newborn babies turned green when they heard me! I hadn't expected the pain to be so horrendous. If I'd only known! I was almost out of my mind, but fortunately the midwife scared me by saying, "If you don't calm down your child won't be born alive!" I tried but didn't do very well. The books don't describe what it's really like.

They probably can't give laughing gas to everyone because they don't have enough people to administer it to every patient.

But it's a relatively simple thing to give laughing gas. The mother herself could administer it.

Yes, perhaps, but there'd have to be someone responsible around; there's always the possibility that something might happen. Here they're always so worried that something will go wrong. And there would have to be a separate person responsible for the gas, aside from the nurse. The patient might be disturbed by another person in the room. You have to consider that hospital services are free, so you can't expect extra comfort. It's possible to buy extra attention and services, that certainly happens, but . . . no, they're always afraid that something might happen, so things are usually left as they are.

Didn't you feel envious of your husband when you had to stay home with the baby for five years while he was out pursuing his artistic career?

Perhaps I did feel envy. But more than that I felt despair. It was as if something had died in me, and I felt paralyzed. I neglected myself—didn't wash or dress or comb my hair. I did everything I was supposed to for my husband and the child— washed, cooked. But I didn't want to do anything else. I would have preferred to die, but the child needed me. I didn't want anything. Anything. It's not unusual. After women give birth, many go into postpartum depression.

As someone who works in Moscow, are you faced with special problems because you're a woman?

Absolutely not. I've never been discriminated against. No one has ever said that there ought to be a man in my place. No, it's the fact that I'm a mother that gets in my way. Of course employers prefer men because . . . if a child is sick the man keeps on working, but the wife has to stay at home. But it isn't all that bad. When the children are about twelve to fifteen years old, the woman can begin to advance.

But fathers also have children?

No, fathers don't have children! If a father stayed at home because his child was sick it would truly be unique. The only possible reason would be if the mother literally couldn't stand on her feet. A lot of prejudices would have to be overcome if the man were to take care of the children while the woman worked. "The old lady supports him," people would say. It's the woman who suffers from that attitude. But of course women share it themselves. "After all, a man is a man," they say.

Do you consider the man's career more important?

That's not the question. The main problem is to find a solution for the children. Institutions, day-care centers, don't live up to their aims. The children who are boarded by the week develop more slowly than children who live at home. They get less attention and they're sick more often. But on the other hand, it does give them a taste of what life will be like in the future.

The birthrate is very low in the Russian Republic and in the three Baltic republics. What do you think can be done to increase it?

That's something I've been very interested in myself. The papers report that most couples want a first child, but in order for people to have a second, better conditions are necessary.

But I think better conditions are more important with the first child. Because it's so hard to take care of the first, it takes an awful lot of strength to have a second one, or even to think about it.

When Alyosha was a baby we had a terribly hard time. I had to fetch water from a well. We lived on my husband's salary—100 rubles a month. We managed because we lived in the country and things were a bit cheaper there. In Moscow we would have starved. During those three years we hardly bought any clothes. I forgot what stockings were; I only had those thick ugly ones. All our money went to buy food; sometimes his parents helped us a little.

I think that part-time work would help everyone. Of course more efficiency would have to be built into the system.

Women work for money, but I know a lot who would work for nothing if only they could get out of the house. To sit at home doing nothing can drive anyone crazy.

Are there any special women's professions here?

Yes. They seem to grow spontaneously. Teaching, for example, has become a woman's profession. I think it's a shame. Men make better teachers than women, but there are hardly any of them.

Why?

The salaries are too low. A man wants at least to appear to support his family. Teaching isn't considered a prestigious job; even an engineer rates higher than a teacher. Selling is another typically female profession. In general, women are in non-mechanized jobs. The subways are staffed with women. They're in jobs that require attention and patience—monotonous jobs. I don't know why teachers, doctors, and cashiers should be so poorly paid while a welder makes between 200 and 300 rubles a month. That's strange! I don't understand the principle behind the system, but it's been with us for a long time. Under Stalin, wages in certain categories were raised when there was no other way of securing labor. But for the worst jobs there always seem to have been enough people.

What does equality between men and women mean to you?

Equality? I don't know. I've never asked myself that question.

According to Soviet law, men and women are equal. Does that work in practice?

Yes, more or less. Sometimes a man has priority, sometimes a woman. If a woman decides to make a career in a so-called man's profession, she can do it, providing she works harder than the men. Equality is written into the law, although the law is seldom invoked. But I'm not terribly upset over the fact that reality and law don't always coincide. The possibility is always there for the woman who wants to push ahead!

In many countries in the West women also have the same rights, technically, as men, but we demand that the law be implemented, and quickly!

In other words you want to use the spurs! We aren't in that much of a hurry. We have to take into consideration our traditions and our huge, very backward countryside.

Don't women here even talk about the inequities between the sexes?

We complain and we argue, but we really don't give each other advice. Each woman solves her own problems. We don't usually turn to the community with problems we can solve at home. There's always some apprehension about turning to the community. It's obligated to take care of the material needs of a child, living conditions, work. But after all, one can't ask the community to come home and educate one's own husband!

And anyway, think of all our organizations! All they really boil down to is paying dues and obligatory attendance. We no longer think that anything can be accomplished by meetings and conferences. We've become immune to that. No, organizations are either illegal or else they don't accomplish a thing. So we prefer to solve our problems quietly and by ourselves.

But we suppose that women are aware that they're treated inequitably—for example, that they receive a lower scale of pay.

Of course. We see . . . a lot. But since we feel powerless, we try not to think about it. Efforts have been made to change conditions, but they've only gotten worse. The consensus is, better leave things as they are. Most people are afraid to express their feelings. Anyone with possible influence would ask themselves a hundred times, "Am I doing the right thing?" There's still a tremendous respect for authority, respect for a government that's here *in spite of* the masses but that at least hasn't gotten worse. Of course we tell stories, gossip, and laugh at what goes on in this country. But what's important is that things aren't as bad as they were.

Salaries may be low, but we're still alive!* Do you see? Inequities don't always give rise to anger. Sometimes they make you subservient.

When you think ahead, what would you like to see happen in your life?

I'd like to have another child. I could support another little one now. Then I want Alyosha to grow up and become a fine human being. I want a good job for my husband, and no further disappointments for him. I wish a good life for everyone. In newspaper interviews women want peace most of all. I do too, and I wish there would be an end to all "ideological differences"—that our country and the West could find a common language. You seem to be able to live with your ideals, and we aren't so badly off either. Why is it necessary to be forever trying to prove that one ideology is better than the other? Perhaps we have much more in common than they want us to know.

Do you think about the future a lot?

Yes, a lot. I think of the future of all of humanity. I want life to continue when I'm gone, when my children are gone.

* Lyuba is making a veiled reference to the mass executions of the Stalin era.

Do you feel that there's a great deal of difference between the kind of life you want to live and your real one?

Well, you know I've had a lot of foolish, un-thought-out ideals. And then of course the difference was enormous. But now . . . I think I really need so little. And I have my so-called inner life! And I do love the world terribly! Somehow I've realized that I understand so little of everything around me, and that it isn't possible to demand that the world be perfect, just for my sake!

The most difficult thing I've had to do was to break with my parents. That has inhibited me a lot. No matter what your mother is like, she's still your mother. To turn against her was the most difficult thing of all, and I had to do it. I still suffer, but I feel I did the right thing.

Finally, I think I'm a fatalist. I feel I have something to accomplish here on earth, and I intend to do it, although I still don't quite know what it is. But you get a certain feeling when you're close to the right thing. I try to do the kind of things that feel close.

What are your immediate plans?

To move my family to the new apartment! After that I'm going away for a month or two to work in a factory where I can fire my ceramics. It's only when I keep on working my things over and over that I finally get what I'm after. So as soon as possible I want to see those two installed. *(She nods in the direction of the other room, where Vitya and Alyosha are playing chess.)* They can get along very well without me. Of course they'll miss me, but now I have to work!

DIVORCES

When the Soviet Union was first established, a very radical law pertaining to the family was passed. Among other things it became easy to dissolve a marriage. It was sufficient for either the husband or the wife to demand one; the formalities were over in a few minutes. In 1936 the laws were amended to require that both parties appear, and in 1944 a law was put on the books that made it difficult, unpleasant, and expensive to be divorced. This law was slightly relaxed in 1965, but where there are children involved, every divorce still has to be tried in court. The court decides, among other things, who is to be in charge of the children, and almost without exception rules in favor of the mother. The father is usually ordered to pay 25 percent of his salary for one child, 33⅓ percent for two, and 50 percent for three or more. It's still very expensive to get divorced; it costs between 50 and 200 rubles depending on whether it's a first divorce or a subsequent one. (A marriage, on the other hand, costs 1 ruble and 50 kopeks.)

Despite the expense, divorces are very common in the Soviet Union. The statistics for 1977 and 1978 show that a third of all marriages end in divorce. In large cities such as Moscow and Kiev half of all marriages are dissolved. Most divorces occur during the first year of marriage.

Why so many divorces? In addition to the usual reasons—alcoholism, physical cruelty, infidelity, etc.—Soviet sociologists have found that about 20 percent of divorces are caused by friction between young couples and their parents and parents-in-law. Of those who divorced in 1977, 79 percent had no place to live when they got married other than with parents or in a communal apartment.

Another contributing factor is the deplorable inadequacy of sex education in the schools. Moreover, it was not until the beginning of the seventies that the first marriage counseling center was opened in Leningrad. In 1976 a doctor who worked at that center said, "I'm not exaggerating when I say that nine-tenths of the young people who are about to get married don't have even a rudimentary knowledge of sex."

N A T A S H A

"FEMININITY IS A CAPACITY FOR INTIMACY,
A TALENT FOR GETTING FLOWERS TO BLOOM."

Natasha and her husband, Yura, live with their one-and-a-half-year-old son in a communal apartment in a very dilapidated house in the center of the city. Their living quarters—a small room with an enormously high ceiling and an unbelievably warped parquet floor—are free. Outside the room is a long, dark corridor that leads to the communal kitchen, where there is a little gas stove, an antiquated sink with a cold-water tap, and baby laundry strung all over the ceiling. At the other end of the corridor is the toilet, a tiny room which consists of a commode without a seat and a floor which is just a couple of boards over a cavernous black hole.

Natasha tells us that her dream for the future is to preside over her own large, clean, light kitchen—without any communal neighbors around.

She is wearing a lightweight salt-and-pepper gray wool dress with a white collar. She has short, well-groomed, dark hair, wears nylon stockings with straight seams, and black, well-polished, low-heeled shoes. She serves food arranged on plates with paper doilies—cakes and cookies, slices of cheese, garlic sausage with lemon wedges and

*freshly chopped chives, herring, fruit and nuts, black and white bread
cut in triangles. With this, Yura serves an amber-colored home-
brewed Georgian vodka that is strong and good.*

*During the interview Natasha is active and present. She leans
forward and speaks quickly and eagerly, seemingly unaware of the
tape recorder in her lap. From time to time Yura comes in, asking
what to feed the baby, where the diapers are, and whether it is the
baby's bedtime yet. Natasha gives quick instructions. When the interview is finished he comes in again, and from that moment it is he
who dominates the conversation. While he pours vodka and talks to
us, Natasha smiles from the corner of the sofa to which she has
retired. Yura has taken her place in the chair opposite us. Several
times we revert to subjects that Natasha has just addressed. Although
we know that her opinions are diametrically opposed to his, she
doesn't open her mouth. It doesn't help that we turn directly to her.
She smiles and remains silent—this despite the fact that she gives us
such a strong feeling of conviction and inner security.*

I'll be twenty-two in May. Right after attending school in
Sverdlovsk in the Urals, I came to the University of Moscow.
That was four years ago. I'm a student at the faculty of law and
will graduate this year. I specialize in criminal law. At first I
was interested only in juvenile crime, but gradually I've become interested in all forms of crime. I'm especially interested
in the social context of crime.

What does your husband do?

He's majoring in mathematics. We'll graduate at the same time,
and then we'll be moving to Akademgorodok.*

* A suburb of Novosibirsk in Siberia, where the Siberian section of the Soviet Union's
Academy of Science is located. Akademgorodok is populated almost exclusively by
scholars and students who work at the university. The standard of education and
research is considered very high.

Have you lived here since you got married?

No. Actually, we could have had a room at the university. Neither Yura nor I have relatives in Moscow, so we really don't have anyplace to live here. We lived at the university until we got married, and it wouldn't have been too difficult to get a room in a two-room apartment there. That would have meant a small private room with shower, toilet, and coat closet shared with the neighbors, and a large communal kitchen— there's one on every floor. But we were tired of living in student rooms. There are always people milling around. And then it was a question of finances. Neither he nor I get much help from home. His parents have four children who have left the nest and need help—three of them live in Moscow. His father is seventy-five and long retired, and his mother retired at fifty-eight, although she still works at a butcher shop to help her children. But we don't get much help since my husband is the oldest child and the others have it worse than we.

My situation is even more complicated because my parents are divorced. My mother is taking care of my brother, who has just finished ninth grade—an age when a child needs a lot of things. My grandmother is seventy, and all she has is her pension. Mama is a pediatrician, but she doesn't make terribly much—no more than 120 rubles per month, or maybe 130 if she works overtime at night. She sends me money, but I try to make her stop. Basically we live on what we earn.

Our grants during our fifth year at the university amount to 45 rubles each, but since we're officially living in a student room, they deduct 6 rubles from our grants each month. And it just isn't possible for three people to live on 84 rubles a month. We've solved the problem in a less than ideal way: Yura works as building superintendent two hours every morning, and sometimes a half day on Saturday. He earns 80 rubles, and we don't have to pay for the room because it comes with the job. It's a large room—25 square meters.

But there are several people living in the apartment, aren't there?

Of course. We considered this when we chose Yura's job. We found a spot where we had friends—some of our classmates live here too—Yura's brother and one of his friends. The three of them arranged to live together. It has its good and bad sides, since I'm the only woman—the others aren't married, so I end up doing the cooking for everybody.

Of course they help with the shopping, but it's still a lot of work. On the other hand it's nice to be the only woman in the kitchen. I can iron and wash and cook when I want to, and there aren't any conflicts. In communal kitchens there are often four women scurrying around, and that creates problems. So in a way I'm lucky.

How long have you lived here?

Not very long. Before this Yura worked as a superintendent in another place. But we were only given an apartment in the basement and it wasn't very suitable for small children. When the baby was really little, things worked out well because we had a small yard where we could put his carriage. But the room was too small and the corridor so drafty that he couldn't play there, and I couldn't keep him in his bed and playpen all day. But we had warm water, and that made things much easier.

You don't have any hot water here?

No, and no bathroom. It's a big problem. I have to heat water for the dishes and the wash. Fortunately there's a public bath not far from here that we use. But we bathe the baby at home and have to heat the water. And the kitchen! Sometimes I visit one of Yura's brothers who lives in a new suburb, and I bathe the baby there. They have a bathroom and a kitchen that are tiny but clean and bright—they're completely white. But this place is horrible!

Where is the baby during the day?

He's with us—as he's always been. Since we don't have anyone else to take care of him, we take turns.

Right before he was born I went home to my mother. I ended up staying there for three months. Because he wasn't very strong and had a little trouble eating when he was born, we don't want to put him in a nursery yet.

Will he go later?

Yes, next year.

Do you think most people think nurseries are a good solution?

No, for the most part people place children in them out of necessity. There are some good ones, especially those connected to factories and institutions; there you don't have to worry about your children. But for the most part nurseries are very bad; the staff is usually very inexperienced and untrained, and turnover is constant. They get minimal wages, the job is taxing, and the groups are far too large—twelve to fifteen children per adult. The children are constantly catching cold because they're always running around in wet diapers. If we were paid for the whole year after having a baby, most women would probably take advantage of it.

What is maternity leave like now?

We get full salary two months before the delivery and two after. Students get a year's leave from the university with a partial grant. But students don't utilize it very often because they fall behind in their studies, and it's hard to manage on a partial grant.

Don't parents usually help?

Yes, they do. When I came to Moscow I had 38 rubles a month and my mother sent me 40. With that I barely got along. If parents didn't help, where would we be?

But what if the parents can't help?

Then the students have to work as watchmen and superintendents. Almost all superintendents here in Moscow are students. Sometimes the work is decently paid, and sometimes a room comes with it. For girls it's harder to get a part-time job.

Isn't it hard to work and study at the same time?

My husband has great problems with that. He never gets all the sleep he needs. It would be easier for me to do a job like his because I'm a morning person.

But we're trying to work and save as much as we can because, now that we're about to embark on careers as academics, we can't go around dressed every which way. Clothes are expensive. Young students can wear what they want, but we have to look a bit more respectable.

Can you tell us what you did yesterday, what an average day is like for you?

First of all, I have to explain something that's unique to me and my husband and that I've hardly ever seen with other people— my husband helps me a lot. We've been able to have a baby without disrupting our plans; it's largely due to him that we were able to finish our studies. He helps me with everything— takes care of the baby, washes and cooks when it's necessary. If I have an exam he's always there to pitch in, and I've always been able to go out knowing that everything will be all right at home. He feeds the baby, puts him to bed, and when I come home everything's in order.

Mornings are always the same. About seven o'clock the baby wakes up and Yura goes to work. Then I feed the baby. I usually put him in a baby chair because I feel he ought to learn to eat by himself. While he sits there and eats, I clean our room, make the bed, and heat the water for the wash. Then I feed him what he didn't finish. He makes an awful mess when he eats, so I have to wash him afterwards. Then, since he's full and happy he plays nicely, and in the meantime I prepare breakfast. While the porridge is cooking I put myself in order. After that I do some washing and ironing, Yura comes home, and we eat.

If Yura has things to do, he leaves. I wash the dishes, play with the baby, take him out, and do things around the house.

The evenings are the busiest time around here. Everyone comes home and has to be fed—at least eight people, because we often have guests. It's hard on me because I have to feed the baby and make dinner for everyone else. Then we take the baby for a walk, put him to bed, wash the dishes, and wash all over again. Things begin to calm down around nine. Then we study as long as we are able. Sometimes I stay up half the night, partly because I have to study, but I also want time to read literature. And sometimes I've borrowed a book that I can only keep for a few days. There are weeks when I sleep only three hours a night, but I don't need much sleep. If Yura has an exam I usually let him have the whole day to himself and I study nights. I find my subject fascinating, and that keeps me going.

We ask Natasha to tell us about her girlhood. She came from a happy, friendly family where her parents truly cared about their children. They took them on long hikes in the woods, read literature, and discussed it with them. When her parents were divorced it was a real crisis for her. She couldn't understand how her father, whom she had always depended on, could suddenly leave the family.

I've always been closer to my father than to my mother. I had a really nice relationship with him—warm and friendly. It was much more complicated with my mother. She was much stricter.

Almost all of my friends were boys, so I mostly played boys' games. Mama, who had been brought up in the old-fashioned way, kept on reminding me that I was a girl and to behave accordingly. But I didn't care for the prim and proper girls she wanted me to emulate.

It's still easier for me to associate with guys. They're more open and straightforward, and to me they're more interesting. Somehow I can't seem to read girls; they're strangers to me. I don't know, maybe I'm more serious than they are. But I know that there are certain feminine characteristics one is supposed to learn in childhood; to be a coquette, to dress well, to devote a lot of time to one's appearance. I never learned any of that. I'm happy with what I have, and don't need anything else. But Yura thinks it's wrong and unfeminine and keeps nagging me to get some nicer things. We used to quarrel about that—especially in the beginning.

I remember when I was fifteen. All the girls were gossiping about who was going to get married first. One girl named Lyalya pointed at me and said, "Natasha will probably never get married. She'll be the baby-sitter for our children." It turned out that I was the first one to get married! Everyone was very surprised.

I've always wanted children—three or four. I know that it's very hard for me to stay at home—after a couple of days I go crazy. But the relationship between Yura and me is such that I don't feel anxious. We'll make out all right.

In educated families there are bound to be conflicts. I recently read a book about Akademgorodok in which the author says, "Nowhere else have I met so many attractive men and so many intelligent women. This is the reason for the high divorce rate there."

Do you understand what I'm getting at? Women who do research, for example, develop the same wish for prestige as men, and since men are used to things being done in a certain way, there are bound to be problems. For men work comes first, then friends and then the wife. But women have to put men first, then the children, and finally their work. Men get prestige from their jobs, women from their children if they're neat and clean.

In our family I believe we're equals. But of course, in a way, Yura is the head of the family . . . because . . . that's the way he wants it. This is the way it works: Officially, outwardly, especially when we're among other people, he's in charge. But in our close family circle, where we decide something between us, we decide it together. But I don't tell this to others, and it's not something I insist on. That could create difficulties, especially if it were known. If people say that the old lady is the boss, everything can go wrong.

Here practically all women work. What happens if a woman always has to give priority to the family?

A woman who has a family has a hard time being accepted into a program of advanced studies. The general consensus is that she won't be able to study and take care of a baby at the same time. But of course this isn't expressed openly. But once in the work force I don't think that those obstacles exist. If she runs into them, it's her own doing. If she has strength and energy and makes the effort and can do her job as well as take care of her home, she won't have any difficulty.

But she does have to manage the two roles simultaneously?

Yes, but nowadays an effort is being made to make things easier for women. In the textile industry, which is almost exclusively a woman's domain, really interesting things are happening. There are services for the employees such as beauty parlors, so that those who work there can go before work or during a break. That makes it easier for women to do their jobs and manage their other chores.

I think it's essential for a woman to work. If I don't work for a period of time, I lose my feeling of self-esteem. It's very important for me to have the intellectual stimulation that work gives me.

But you wouldn't consider not having a child?

No, I can't possibly think of a life without a child. As I said, I'd like to have three or four, but I definitely plan to have two.

Most people here have only one child. How come?

The low standard of living!

What do you think of the Hungarian system, which allows women to stay home for three years?

I don't believe in it. To stay at home for one year is bad enough. But three! What does a woman get out of those years?

In our country [Sweden] the man can also stay at home.

Oh, that sounds fantastic! Then one doesn't have to be alone— that's the hardest part.

No, only one at a time can stay at home.

Oh, I see. Then that would never work here. Our men don't operate that way. For them children don't exist until they're around two. That's when they start playing with them, taking them for walks, and teaching them one thing and another. When our baby was three months old my husband had no idea how to care for him. A baby for most men is a completely alien thing, just a lump of flesh.

You can't imagine a man working in a day nursery?

Definitely not. I guess it's traditional thinking, but I feel that women are more orderly, more meticulous. They do everything more carefully. In dealing with children that's of the essence. Patience is also terribly important, and men don't have much of that. And then, of course, there's the cooking. A man may prepare something from time to time, for special occasions, but to make the food every day—they'd never be able to take it!

In hotels and subways only women do the cleaning. Is that because they have patience?

Of course not. The snobbery of men is the decisive factor. Sometimes Yura protests, "Why should I do this kind of job. I'm a man!" And really, service jobs are women's work. The man is the hunter. It's he who makes the money.

Then you must also feel that parents play entirely different roles in the family.

Yes, a good mother first of all has to have patience and be able to keep herself and the child clean. Cleanliness is very important and demands both strength and energy. It eliminates a lot of problems. Also, a mother must have inner peace; she must be able to control herself, otherwise both she and the child can be hurt. But she mustn't hover and be overprotective. She has to be calm and patient but also bold.

And a good father?

Yura is a good father. He really spends time with the boy. It's especially important for a boy to have contact with his father. There are a lot of masculine characteristics that a boy picks up from his father, and that's what Yura is giving to our boy, the ability to take risks, to be courageous, for example. A mother is by nature more cautious, and a boy who grows up only with women is more easily frightened.

Do you think you manage to be a good mother?

Yes, I think so. And lots of people have told me that I've become a good mother. I'm pleased that I don't get upset with the baby, whatever happens. I've never become hysterical or flared up; if I stay calm I can always find a solution. I always control myself for his sake.

Do you think that boys and girls ought to be brought up differently for the different roles that await them?

Yes, absolutely! There are certain things boys ought to learn and others that girls ought to learn. Since I don't think that household work has anything to do with equality of the sexes but is a practical family arrangement, I think that girls ought to learn about household chores at a very early age, so that they can do things quickly and efficiently and not spend too much time on them. I've never learned as I should have. It always takes me a long time to prepare a meal, and now I have to do such a lot of cooking. As I said, the other people who live here are all men, and they demand meat every day. They're also spoiled, and I can't let them fill up on porridge. If there were only the three of us I'd prepare a soup that would last for several days, but now that there are so many of us, our largest pot isn't big enough. I couldn't even make enough soup if I stood in the kitchen half a day.

Shouldn't boys learn to do those kinds of chores?

Of course, but not to the same extent. A boy needs to learn how to do the essential things so that he can take care of himself. A girl has to know much more. Aside from that she should know how to sew and knit—the earlier she learns, the easier life will be. In the same way, boys have to learn something about carpentry, how to hang things on the wall, and how to find solutions to different problems.

You said that you hadn't learned to be feminine. Is that something one can learn?

I don't know. Many think of femininity as the ability to dress well, be attractive to the opposite sex—things like that. But I see femininity as kindness, sincerity, gentleness, the touch of the artist, a capacity for intimacy, a talent for getting flowers to bloom. Femininity is *also* the ability to express oneself, but without such subterfuge as coquetry, which is coarse and vulgar. A woman's face ought to have an expression of inner, ethereal beauty, and every woman ought to be romantic deep down. There's a proverb that I see as an allegory about women in general: When a woman expects a child, she ought to sit at the window and look at a beautiful landscape, or read beautiful stories. Then she'll have a beautiful child. So, femininity is inner, not outer beauty.

I've recently been reflecting on which qualities a man ought to have and which a woman ought to have, and I've come to the conclusion that they're basically the same qualities—intelligence, compassion, and strength—but that they're expressed in different ways, with different nuances. Even strength is something different for a man and a woman. Obviously, I'm talking about emotional, not physical strength. A man has to be strong enough to make decisions, fast decisions, to persevere, to resolve certain problems and conflicts that arise within the family. A woman's strength consists of putting her imprint on her family and almost unnoticeably—very gently—creating a spiritual atmosphere. Feminine strength is once again a question of patience—sometimes to know how to keep one's mouth shut and stay out of conflict.

You say that men and women ought to be strong in different ways. Doesn't that create inequality within the community?

Yes, I've noticed that, especially where women are concerned, the characteristics I was just describing are different from those needed in professional life. Of course, this can lead to personality conflicts. I have a friend who is tender and gentle, a dreamer. But as a teacher she's forced to be hard and severe. This is a difficult problem for her, so the problem you are alluding to does exist. Unfortunately, here one's choice of profession seldom coincides with one's inner nature. It depends on a decision made by one's parents, or the family situation in general; or perhaps the individual quite simply can't decide what to do and doesn't have the time to consider the choice carefully. The fact that a woman's inner qualities sometimes conflict with the way she has to behave at work is, in my opinion, one of the principal causes of neuroses.

To discover that she isn't suited to a particular job is a greater problem for a woman than for a man, because it's harder for a woman to start all over again. It's the same thing within the family. The woman is more faithful and has a harder time breaking the relationship. Even if she no longer loves her husband, she has a hard time leaving him—for practical reasons as well. So she compromises.

What do you mean by practical reasons?

It's harder for her to get by. It's harder for a woman to get a part-time job, and then she has the child to care for.

Doesn't custody ever go to the husband?

No. The woman always has care of the child. Only if she's sick or severely alcoholic does she lose her right as a mother.

Do you think that's right?

Of course. The mother is always closer to the child.

We've heard of instances where a woman refuses to grant a divorce.

That's true. But in that case the man simply takes off to another city and starts a new life there with another woman. When they've lived together for a couple of years he gets his divorce. But of course it can be a terrible situation. For a woman with children it's difficult to find someone to marry, especially if she's a bit on in years.

What do you mean by "on in years"?

When she's around thirty-five to forty life becomes difficult for her. At about thirty here she begins to get fat and to lose her glow. This is quite natural. Her home, her family, and her job leave her no time for herself.

You say that it's easier for men to walk out on their marriages than it is for women. Is infidelity common?

I know that there's hardly a man who can manage to be faithful. That of course goes for my husband as well. It would be a serious problem only if he really fell in love with someone else. But if it isn't a tragedy for the other woman and doesn't mean anything to him, I can very well forgive him.

How would he react if you were unfaithful?

I think it would devastate him. He can't even imagine my becoming interested in another man.

Lately, Yura and I have had some heated discussions about what a woman ought to be. We've even quarreled about it. I feel that many people put women down. It's not considered important for a woman to be intelligent. If a woman runs the household well and is attractive, it doesn't matter too much if she's stupid. An intelligent woman can cause problems. It may sound like bragging, but my husband sometimes suffers terribly! If a woman argues with her man and questions his opinions, life will be more difficult for him.

Yura and I don't have problems as far as the household is concerned. Our problems are on another level. We sometimes have different opinions. Usually, a woman agrees with her husband, convinced of his superiority—his strength and intelligence. She denies her own opinions and accepts his politics and his general views on life.

What are your points of difference?

About women's role, or rather women's *place* in society, I should say. Yura feels that if a woman is married and has children, her family should come first and everything else should take second place. I don't feel that one can divide things up like that.

For instance, if I'm invited to do something with friends, should I say no because of Yura, or should I have the right to go? If Yura is depressed, of course I'd stay at home. One must be considerate toward one's husband. But he has to reciprocate.

Even if we've quarreled and disagreed, he now lets me go. But there's conflict and pain involved. If I borrow a book for a certain number of days and there are things in the house that can wait, he thinks it's O.K. that I put them off and read instead. On those occasions he might even help me.

I think that a woman has a right—even an obligation—to think of her own development. It's important for the happiness of the family that the woman care about her outer as well as her inner self. If not, the man stops caring for her; she's no longer the person he married.

What dreams and wishes do you have right now?

Right now all we can think about is what it's going to be like when we move to Akademgorodok—we're so much looking forward to living there, and we feel tremendously lucky to have been posted there.

Akademgorodok is a city of small, low houses in the middle of the forest. Mostly "classy" people live there—or students and professors, at any rate. There are beautiful woods with lots of squirrels running around. I'm used to living in the country, and I'm dying to move there. And the work will certainly be interesting. Yura and I will work near each other. To start out we'll have a student apartment with a communal kitchen, but after two or three years we'll get our own apartment.

Then your hopes will be realized fairly soon?

Well, I don't know for sure that everything will work out as well as we hope. But in any case we think we'll be able to work in our professions and to live better. We're so tired of always having people around us. We need to have a place of our own and to be able to have guests. And I have a humble little wish of my own: to have my own kitchen, one that's peaceful and clean and has hot water. We also wish we had a pile of money so that we'd be able to do the things we want, not only work but hobbies. Yura is very fond of carpentry. I love nature and to tramp around in the woods. I used to draw, but I had to give it up. We'd like to take our vacations together, to travel, live in a tent, go canoeing. . . .

Maybe it's because I'm so tired right now, or because of all the difficulties we've had, but it seems to me that I've become very passive. Sometimes I want nothing more than to rest, to be by myself. For both of us the ideal is to inspire each other. We don't always succeed, though.

What makes our marriage work is that Yura helps me so much. What's bad about it is our astonishing ability to hitch on to problems that don't really exist. We can fly off the handle over the most unimportant things. But after all, he's an Armenian. He was brought up with an ultraconservative view of women, which he's having a hard time divorcing himself from, even though I'm fighting hard against it. He has to be the one who decides. His interests have to take precedence over mine. He has to stand over me, and even if we come to a decision together he seems to want me to be subservient. But my feeling is that things won't continue that way.

How is life for women in general? Does equality really exist in the Soviet Union?

There's equality on the social level. Women have the same basic rights and freedoms as men do, including the right to choose their profession. But no laws are strong enough to penetrate the family. Our upbringing, habits, and traditions have such deep roots that that kind of equality just isn't possible. And the basic physiological differences between men and women are just too great to allow for complete equality. What there can be is a kind of reasonable equality that acknowledges that only a woman can give birth to a child.

Do you think there's a great deal of difference between Soviet women and women in the West?

That's hard to say. I think women here are less pressured by a conception of what life ought to be. We don't talk so much about what others do and how they manage their lives. So there are greater opportunities here to listen to one's own impulses and to develop freely.

Let's say that two families live in an apartment. The first family can buy anything they wish, while the other can't make ends meet. It would be pretty hard for the second family. Perhaps they wouldn't exactly feel ashamed, but they would be unhappy, and they might start buying things that they couldn't really afford. It's my impression that in your society a lot of people have such a good standard of living that they make people around them jealous. They set examples that actually serve to oppress people and give them inferiority complexes.

Do you think that a women's movement is needed here?

No, I don't think so. It wouldn't be permitted. Here decisions are made through political organizations, elected representatives in the work place to whom people can turn. I don't think anything could be solved by a separate women's movement, but only through organizations at the local level.

How can changes be worked into the family?

Changes certainly ought to take place in the home, but I don't know how. Right now the attitude of most men is "Woman, *you* take care of the household! Hand me the newspaper." How could this possibly be changed by a few decrees?

But everything is moving toward change in a gradual way, in part because women are becoming more aware of questions of equality as they become more educated. Perhaps individual women can gradually change the masculine attitude. Not by screaming and crying and being hysterical, but by logical proof that this is true and that is true and there it is in black and white.

These aren't decrees. I don't think that decrees will change anything.

T A N Y A

"EACH ONE OF US HAS TO ADJUST
THE BEST SHE CAN."

*e met Tanya at a designated spot in the subway. She
and her husband, Dima, come straight toward us. No
one can fail to notice our foreign clothes.*

*From the subway we transfer to a bus. Long before
we manage to get out our five-kopek coins, Dima has paid for all of
us. The noise and commotion make it almost impossible to talk.
When we get to their stop, they make a sign to get off, and we push
our way through the crowd. Dima gets off first and courteously helps
us off. Then we zigzag across streets and yards between yellow and
green wooden houses—yet another surprisingly countrylike area right
in the center of the big city. Between the houses, trees have been
planted so close together and so haphazardly that they look as if they
were growing there long before the houses were built.*

*At the entrance to the house there is a sign stating that the occu-
pants are to be commended for being careful and clean. Tanya and
Dima don't share in this honor; we're on our way to a borrowed
apartment. Tanya and Dima live with her family, and we would
disturb them there.*

I was born in Moscow, have lived here all my life. I'm twenty-four years old. I now work as a teacher of sociology at an institute here. You've already met my husband, who is still studying. My parents are economists. They're retired but they both still work. I also have an older sister who is married and has a child.

We live together with my family in a two-room apartment, forty square meters in size. We have one room, my parents the other. It's a good apartment in an old house, centrally located, but also near a green area. It's a nice place to live.

Of course, it's difficult to live with an older couple. We always have to consider that they need to rest more than we do. When we want to invite people over, we generally ask beforehand whether it's convenient for my parents. And we live in tight quarters. We have room for only one desk in our room, and it's hard for both of us to work there at the same time. But I don't think these problems are major; they're nothing to get depressed about. We'll find some solution, but since we have what is considered a lot of space for four persons, it's not possible at the moment. But they've promised that the housing problem will be solved by 1980.*

My childhood was probably quite typical of everyone who grew up in this country. Perhaps we were a little better off economically than most others. I also had the advantage that my mother practically never worked outside the home when I was young. She gave me everything she could. I'm very grateful, and I hope to be able to do the same for my children.

I went to an ordinary school, not too bad, although there probably were better ones. I played in an orchestra, studied languages, did sports—figure skating. It wasn't a special school, but I didn't need any extra tutoring to get into the university—I got along with what I learned in school.

Papa was really a secondary influence in my childhood. He didn't concern himself much with me, and I never had any

* This statement of Tanya's was probably wishful thinking. The housing problem has not yet been solved.

conflicts with him. He supported me while Mama stayed at home. Mama and I were together so much that we understood each other without speaking. We never argued, and now that I'm an adult I can talk to her about everything. But sometimes I don't feel like talking, and then she doesn't ask. She waits until I open up.

I've never wished that I had been a boy, but I don't know how different things would have been. But now that I'm mature I see that men have an easier time of it in a lot of ways. But I also think that the problems we have with men have been caused by women themselves. We women brought them up like that. We reap what we sow.

Although I'm married, I'm still a child in certain respects. I think it's because we live at home with my parents. Everything Mama did for me she now does for both of us. She works full time as an insurance agent and makes calls when people are at home. It's hard work because there's so much footwork involved, and she has to do a lot of talking. But since she works irregular hours, it's easier for her to shop than it is for me. So usually she's the one who both shops and does the cooking. This also has to do with the fact that she's always been a housewife, and two housewives in one household just wouldn't work. So she continues, but of course I help more than I used to. Dima and I do about the same amount, but between Papa and Mama she does most of the work in the house. They got married forty years ago, and it just happened that way.

Dima and I don't have children yet; we've been married only a year and want to wait until Dima has completed his studies so that we'll have an easier time financially. Right now our parents are helping us. Our decision to wait has to do with my ideas about motherhood. I want to bring up my child myself —I don't want my Grandfather or Grandmother to do it. I want to raise my child the way my mother raised me, but as of this moment there's no way for me to arrange my life so that I can stay home. There are also other things that interest me more right now. But I do want children! The relationship between people can't stagnate; it has to grow. I'm against having children immediately, but if one waits, the child will be a joy and will complete the relationship. I can't imagine life without that joy.

I'd like to have three children. But we'll have only one, perhaps two. We couldn't give more children than that what we'd like to give them, nor could we realize our own plans and wishes. And I don't think that one ought to subjugate oneself to one's children. A good mother develops her own potential to the utmost. Then there's the apartment situation. We can't possibly have children in the present circumstances; I don't want to burden our parents endlessly. But we may be able to have our first child in five or six years.

Right now I wish I had more time for my work. I guess it's a question of my own laziness and the difficulty I have in organizing my time. But I don't go around dreaming about what I can't have. Of course I wish for a month's vacation in the sun and our own apartment. But if I expect to succeed, it depends on me.

How do you see the woman's role here?

A woman ought to have style and good taste. She should be gentle and feminine. Looks aren't important, but she has to be well-groomed. And she has to be outwardly oriented. I don't mean only on the job, but also at home and in her appearance. She can't let things like that slide. They're important not only for the outward impression they make but also for the woman's own sense of self. If she's well-dressed, she feels better able to deal with her problems.

A woman ought not to be totally dependent on her husband for everything, but should have something of her own. She should blend dependence and independence. If she can relate well to other people without being too vulnerable, that's close to the ideal.

If we have a girl, I'd like to bring her up the way I was brought up, except that we'd want to give her more independence and a greater feeling of freedom. I'd like her to be sensitive toward others, but less vulnerable than I am. On the moral plane I'd want to impose the same rules I had to follow: Conduct yourself so that you don't hurt others. Be helpful to other people. Be sensitive and good.

If we had a boy I would probably ask the advice of my mother-in-law. She had such success with hers!

Now Tanya starts to question us. She laughs as if she is afraid that her questions might sound stupid. "Do you have day-care centers? Are they state operated? Do people willingly put their children there? How many children in a group?"

We ask her: How are things here? You've said that you'd prefer to be home when the children are small.

Of course, unless I could get them into a good day-care center where they could learn English, and then I'd enroll them there. But if I could only get them into an ordinary day-care center I'd prefer to stay at home with them until they were around five.

With the job I have now I could manage. But if I were forced to choose between continuing to work and staying at home, we'd have to find a solution. But I wouldn't want to have a substitute mother. I think that the child's upbringing starts the first week of its life. One immediately starts building a relationship, learning the child's needs, what to do and what not to do. A substitute mother, no matter how capable, is still not the real mother.

How do you feel about abortions?

I have no special feelings about them. In talking with other women I've been made to realize that psychologically they're more difficult for someone who has already had children than for those who haven't. So far I haven't had an abortion—knock on wood.

Is abortion used as a kind of birth control?

No, as far as I know, all women try to avoid abortion because it's so terribly painful. But there must be ways of making it less so. There isn't enough work done in this area, nor in birth control. The attitude toward birth control has changed much later here than in the West, and we're behind you. The perfect method hasn't been found anywhere, and there hasn't been enough research done.

Here, of course, it's all tied into society's attitude. Perhaps the reasoning goes something like this: We have too low a birthrate, and if we are going to let people decide whether to have children or not . . . Perhaps that's the reason no research is done in this field. But there has to be a breakthrough. Women can't continue to be plagued by this.

Of course conditions are better than before. A family can usually manage with one child. But the higher standard of living is also one of the reasons for the lower birthrate. The demand for material goods has increased, and the desire to give one's children a good education has kept pace with that. But that's usually not possible before one is in one's thirties and has achieved a so-called stable life.

Women seem to be making some progress: We've been promised more and better day-care centers. They're also talking about longer maternity leaves after birth, which of course will have the effect of encouraging a higher birthrate. The government has become aware of the problem, and that's already something. The birthrate, of course, is a social problem, not a psychological one, as some have insisted. It's said that women's innate sense of motherhood has been lost, but that isn't the case at all.

Would day-care centers be better if men worked there?

Of course—if he had a woman next to him to change the baby, feed it, etc. A man can't seem to manage things like that very well. I can imagine a man in a day-care center but not in a nursery.

You said that a man has an easier life than a woman in many ways. What did you mean by that?

Their professional life is easier. Their psyche permits them to push away the problems that exist at home and perform their jobs in peace, without outside interference. I'm of course referring to intellectual work, since I don't know any other. It's harder for a woman to follow such a course. But on the other hand, if a woman wants to, then she can accomplish much more than a man because she has more perseverance.

Are there any occupations that you would consider typical for women?

No, I don't think so.

Doctors, teachers—aren't they mostly women?

Yes, but I think that's wrong. Our history, our literature point out that men are much better than women as doctors and teachers. I don't know why, but I do know that my men teachers were always much better than the women.

Do men and women aspire to different goals?

A goal is expressed in the demands that are put on a person, and these demands in turn determine what that person's role in society is. Man has his, woman has hers. If one assumes this as a premise, then men and women have different goals. But they can also be similar. Both can be career-oriented. But often part of man's social role is to make progress in his professional life. Therefore one could say that if a woman has "made it," she's accomplished more than a man, because the demands on her have been greater.

By different demands do you mean that a woman has to work harder to achieve higher goals?

Yes, she has to be more persevering, more capable, just better. That isn't typical only of our society. It's the same everywhere. Women have to work much harder than men. Even when a man and a woman have the same position at work and the same high standing in the community, one can assume that the woman in question is more gifted, because she has been forced to accomplish considerably more in order to get to that point. A woman has a hard time in the work force because she has to compete with men. Since she has children, she's not considered desirable as an employee. A child who's sick creates a problem for her. A man can always be on the job and is considered more reliable, so if there's a choice between a man and a woman, the man will always be chosen. From the economic point of view, of course, it is always more desirable to employ the man. But what about from the moral point of view?

In Sweden we try to solve this by giving the father paternity leave as well.

That would be difficult here because men advance faster on the job than women and their jobs tend to be more responsible. So a scheme like that probably wouldn't be feasible here.

But isn't that unfair? Shouldn't there be an effort to change the system somehow? •

At the moment I don't think it's possible, not with the present social structure.

Do you think there will be a change in the future?

Yes, probably. But one thing is sure—housework will continue to impede and hinder women's progress for the next hundred years. No matter how much community services improve, it will still be women who have to assume that responsibility.

And as long as no real solutions are offered, each one of us has to adjust the best she can according to her own possibilities and resources.

Would it be inconceivable to have a women's movement here of the type we have in the West?

We're so different from you. We aren't active. We've been taught to leave our problems to the government. The government thinks for us, takes care of us. Maybe we relegate too much responsibility. The government isn't God, after all, and can't be all-encompassing. Perhaps we ought to be a little more active, but I don't know how. We don't discuss our problems the same way you do. We can, of course, turn to our representatives. But you can hardly go to your representative and tell him that you want to write your dissertation but that you have two children who need to be cared for. There are more serious problems—the lack of housing, for example.

Do women admit that their situation is a difficult one, or do they have guilt feelings about their "failures" both as mothers and in the work force?

Of course they take on the guilt themselves! There's a terrible feeling of frustration among women. They're unsatisfactory as mothers and inadequate at their work. I haven't gone through it yet, but I can see what a dilemma it is.

In our circumstances I think the most important ingredient is our will. The conflict between children and a job has to be overcome on a personal level. And only the woman herself can do that.

POSTSCRIPT

Soviet women live in a society where it's taken for granted that a woman should be educated and have a profession, and where there is also guaranteed employment. Women in the Soviet Union aren't exploited by the same ruthless and alienating commercialism as in the West, and they escape being used as sex objects for commercial and pornographic purposes.

The Soviet woman lives in a society where relationships between people often are closer and stronger than in the West, and where family ties—partly because the generations still are dependent on each other—prevent the loneliness and isolation that are so prevalent among us.

The fact that the women we interviewed so rarely emphasize these positive aspects of their lives suggests that they take them so much for granted that they hardly seem worthy of interest. When, for example, we described the low level of self-esteem that is so characteristic of women in the West and that we interpret as a consequence, among other things, of incongruities in the capitalist system, the Soviet women had no idea what we were talking about. We ended up admiring the strong self-assurance of these women.

Why, then, is the picture of women's conditions in the Soviet Union that the interviewees present so bleak?

"Equality between women and men—what does it mean?" we asked Lyuba. After a moment's hesitation she answered, "Equality? I don't know. I've never asked myself that question."

What does her answer really mean? All the women we spoke to—including Lyuba—actually had very definite opinions about equality, women's problems, and sex roles. But it turned out that these opinions were riddled with contradictions—precisely as if these women had "never asked themselves that question." Sometimes these contradictions were an indication that they weren't used to talking about or analyzing the problems. We were amazed that women who talked about obvious inequities could at the same time deny that these inequities were worth discussing with other women.

We also came to see the contradictions as an expression of an almost schizophrenic concept of reality: On the one hand, the women often assured us that they were fully equal to men; and on the other, they talked, not only indirectly and unconsciously, but also in direct and straightforward terms, about how they suffered from belonging to the "second sex" in the male-oriented Soviet Union. This split perception of reality, which occurred with such frequency, seems to have its origins in two myths: that Soviet women are equal to Soviet men, and that women need to be "feminine." We had expected to encounter both these conceptions, but we thought we would find a dividing line between official and private ideologies; we never imagined that the myth of equality would be embraced to almost the same degree by individual women as by the official ideology, nor did we imagine that the myth of femininity would be encouraged so consistently by society as a whole.

During the early days of the Soviet Union there was a strong political desire to come to terms with all forms of discrimination against women. But despite great ideological and practical efforts, not the least of which were made by Aleksandra Kollontai, the existing economic conditions made the actual chances of accomplishing the liberation of women very small. The value of a carefully thought-out strategy for women's questions was minimized, and it is significant that when Clara Zetkin* asked Lenin to write something about sexual and family education he replied, "Further ahead—not yet! Now all my strength and time have to go into other issues. There are greater, more serious problems."

But with the enormous economic changes that the Soviet Union has undergone since then, shouldn't these obstacles have been cleared away a long time ago? Why has the emancipation of women been so long in coming?

There was also at that time a firm belief in the doctrine that a woman in a Communist society would automatically be equal. Marx and Engels were interpreted as saying that the abolition of personal property would mean that the woman "regained" the equality she had possessed at the dawn of mankind's history. This would constitute part of a historical process regulated by law.

So the orthodox Marxist doctrine came to be that independent women's organizations were superfluous: The class struggle would lead to socialism and thereby to the emancipation of women. In 1920 Lenin said to Clara Zetkin, "Now all Communist women, all working women, have to concentrate on the revolution of the proletariat, which will also build a foundation for the necessary renewal of conditions for marital and sexual relationships."

By the end of the 1920s, with the growing influence of Stalinism, it became unthinkable to question Marxist doctrines. For women this meant that the theory of automatic equality in socialist society gradually was elevated to the status of fact. In the Soviet Union the state had taken over the means of production; therefore, the Soviet woman was equal to the Soviet

* Clara Zetkin (1857–1933) was a leading German Communist, one of the principal founders of the German Communist Party, and a leader of the right-wing, Russophile element of that party.

man. As a result, the Zhenotdel—the section within the Party that since 1919 had concentrated specifically on women's questions—was dissolved in 1930. The fact that Soviet women haven't been permitted to organize independent organizations since then has certainly contributed to the present state of affairs.

It is true that women in the Soviet Union today are gainfully employed in larger numbers than in perhaps any other country. At the same time, however, because of their double work load and the traditional sex-role attitudes they encounter (and express themselves), they are discriminated against in the work force. Against this background one can't help being surprised that the contrast between women's rights according to the law and their limited abilities to take advantage of these rights hasn't destroyed the myth of equality.

Naturally there are reasons for this, at least one of them historical. During World War II, 25 million people died in the Soviet Union—most of them men. The surplus of women after the war was enormous, and women needed all their strength for their own and their children's survival. Women had to replace men in heavy reconstruction work, so it was not surprising that later on, when things normalized, women longed for a partial return to the old sex roles. Nor did the conservative family policies of the 1950s promote women's liberation or the breaking of traditions that had lasted for centuries.

The ideology of equality that the Soviet Union embraces is based on "biological" thinking, which helps to explain why the myth of equality has become so entrenched. Not only the physical differences between the sexes but also the psychological ones are considered to be biologically determined. In other words, Soviet sociologists and experts on women's questions believe that the demand for equality must be tempered by the basic differences between the sexes—which means, in plain language, that women are not only physically weaker than men but also have psychological characteristics that make them less suitable for certain "demanding" assignments. In this way the consequences of biological thinking become a permanent impediment to improving women's place in the work force.

Even though the means of production have been taken over by the Soviet state, there hasn't been any change in a work pattern originally set up by men for men. The places of work, the factories, the machines—as well as the attitudes—are the same as before. But since women are "different" (i.e., "lesser"), this lack of change is something no one calls attention to. Quite the contrary—every time a woman can't adjust to some aspect of working life, the fault lies with her, not in the way the work is organized. And we know the consequences: Women and men choose different professions, women's jobs are more poorly paid and have lower status than men's, male competitiveness is allowed to crowd out women, having a child becomes a liability—and for women, "women's conflicts" and the fact that they don't feel at home in the work place are accepted as inevitable. "The fact that a woman's inner qualities sometimes conflict with the way she has to behave at work is one of the principal causes of neuroses, I believe," says Natasha. And in her "has to behave" there is no irony, only resignation.

Of course this biological train of thought has consequences not only in professional life. The fact that women give birth to and nurse babies is also used as proof that they have primary and self-evident responsibility not only for the children but also for the housework. This very household work (which Lenin described as "barbaric, unproductive, petty, enervating, stupefying, and depressing") was something from which the socialist state was going to liberate women. But the dissolution of private ownership hasn't dissolved the family as an economic entity; and the household still hasn't been transformed into the communal responsibility that Engels once envisaged.

Since Lenin's negative description of household drudgery had a terribly strong impact on Soviet society for such a long time, it is almost frighteningly ironic that even now so little has been done to relieve women of their double duty. But of course Hilda Scott is right when she says in her book *Does Socialism Liberate Women?*, "It is doubtful whether anyone in Lenin's time had calculated what it would require to take housework out of the home and put it on an efficient, workable basis in an industrial society. . . . Even when the best intentions are present, there must also be an *economic base* sufficiently strong and well-organized to assume these economic functions. At the same time there must be a *theoretical concept* and a *plan of action*. So far no socialist country has met these conditions" (our italics).

Today the Soviet Union still talks about expanded social services as the most important solution to women's problems. At the same time it is obvious that a change in the official ideology has been allowed to justify the slow development of community service: "A good woman is also a good housewife," booms Brezhnev in newspaper editorials. "But one thing is sure," Tanya says. "Housework will impede and hinder women's progress for another hundred years." That any change is very far off seems quite certain.

The myth that women are equal leads to passivity when they are faced with inequities—a passivity that is strengthened by the myth of femininity that is apparently shared by everyone. All the women we interviewed unhesitatingly described what being feminine means to them: A woman is soft, agreeable, patient, caring, unselfish. . . . The concept of femininity has a clear and positive meaning to them, and it seems to give them a strong sense of identity; undoubtedly this is one of the reasons they radiate such security and self-assurance in their role as women.

But self-assurance alone doesn't bring about freedom from oppression. For one thing, the Soviet conception of femininity doesn't have any cultural or social overtones—there is no conscious attempt to establish a female culture or to give equal weight to the feminine aspects of society. Instead, the conservative sex-role model is the one that is persistently reinforced in schools, cultural life, and the mass media. Secondly, the community and the work place are almost exclusively dominated by male standards and ideals, and here feminine qualities are transformed into something like weaknesses that can be exploited. Despite the feeling of self-assurance that the woman gets from having a professional life, a conflict often arises between her feminine ideals and the limited opportunities to realize them that the Soviet system offers. It isn't easy to be "soft, calm, patient, and beautiful" when one has to struggle with a double work load, stress, long lines, lack of merchandise, preoccupation with the children, and a difficult financial situation. How does one, for example, reconcile the conception that "a good mother should give her child some kind of spiritual guidance," with circumstances that force her to put him in a day-care center five days and nights a week?

As the interviews show, all these contradictory demands on women do cause conflict. Even if the women rarely explained *why* their situation was unfair, they agreed, almost without exception, that it *was*. But when we looked for the desire for change, suggestions for solutions, a unified stand among women and a fighting spirit—what did we find? Almost none of these. It may seem callous to ask for struggle and protest in a country where the opportunities for such action are so much more restricted than in ours. But we seldom found even indignation. For each and every woman, the solution for the time being was private and individual. It was a matter of having a grandmother who was willing to care for the child, or a question of having money or "contacts." But most of all it was a question of being able to endure. The social solutions they could imagine were somewhere in the distant future, and they were the traditional ones: Men have to start helping, the society has to expand services, women should have larger subsidies for children and longer maternity leaves.

Their attitude was one of resignation. Maybe things would start to move in the right direction—the government was, after all, "aware of the problems." One just had to wait and see.

FURTHER READING

Atkinson, Dorothy, et al., eds. *Women in Russia.* Stanford, Calif.: Stanford University Press, 1977.

Bronfenbrenner, Urie. *Two Worlds of Childhood: U.S. and U.S.S.R.* New York: Russell Sage Foundation, 1970.

Chao, Paul. *Women Under Communism: Family in Russia and China.* Bayside, N.Y.: General Hall, 1977.

Jacoby, Susan. *Inside Soviet Schools.* New York: Schocken Books, 1974.

Kollontai, Alexandra. *Alexandra Kollontai: Selected Writings.* Alix Holt, editor and translator. Westport, Conn.: Lawrence Hill, 1978.

Lapidus, Gail Warshofsky. *Women in Soviet Society: Equality, Development, and Social Change.* Berkeley: University of California Press, 1978.

Lapidus, Gail Warshofsky, ed. *Women, Work, and Family in the Soviet Union.* Vladimir Talmy, translator. Armonk, N.Y.: M. E. Sharpe, 1981.

Mamonova, Tatyana, ed. *Women in Russia.* Boston: Beacon Press, 1983.

Mandel, William M. *Soviet Women*. Garden City, N.Y.: Ramparts Press, 1975.

Sacks, Michael Paul. *Women's Work in Soviet Russia: Continuity in the Midst of Change*. New York: Praeger Publishers, 1976.

Scott, Hilda. *Does Socialism Liberate Women? Experiences from Eastern Europe*. Boston: Beacon Press, 1974.

Smith, Hedrick. *The Russians*. New York: Quadrangle/New York Times Books, 1976.

Stites, Richard. *The Women's Liberation Movement in Russia: Feminism, Nihilism, and Bolshevism, 1860–1930*. Princeton, N.J.: Princeton University Press, 1978.

Trotsky, Leon. *Women and the Family*, rev. ed. Max Eastman et al., translators. New York: Pathfinder Press, 1973.

ABOUT THE AUTHORS

Both natives of Sweden, Carola Hansson and Karin Lidén have taken advantage of their proximity to the Soviet Union to visit it many times, and have long been interested in the position of women in that country. In addition to their collaboration on *Moscow Women,* they have translated material written by exiled Leningrad feminists for a book that was published in Sweden in 1981.

At present, Carola Hansson works as a dramatist for Swedish television and lives with her husband and four children in Uppsala. Karin Lidén works as a consultant and writer for Swedish radio and lives with her husband and child in Paris.

Gail Warshofsky Lapidus, who wrote the Introduction, is head of Berkeley's Center for Slavic and East European Studies and the author of *Women in Soviet Society.*

WOMEN'S STUDIES IN PAPERBACK FROM PANTHEON

The Charlotte Perkins Gilman Reader:
The Yellow Wallpaper and Other Fiction
edited by Anne Lane (1980)
A collection of the work of the nineteenth-century feminist.
0-394-73933-7 $4.95

Eve and the New Jerusalem:
Socialism and Feminism in the Nineteenth Century
by Barbara Taylor (1983)
"A breathtakingly detailed recovery of a lost chapter in the
history of socialism and feminism."
—Elaine Showalter
0-394-71321-4 $9.95

Herland: *A Lost Feminist Utopian Novel*
by Charlotte Perkins Gilman (1979)
Herland describes a society of women discovered by three male
explorers who then must re-examine their assumptions about women
and their roles in society. "A pure delight . . . a serendipitous discovery."
—Susan Brownmiller
0-394-73665-6 $2.95

Moscow Women: *Thirteen Interviews*
by Carola Hansson and Karin Lidén (1983)
Lively, candid, and often moving interviews with women
from the Soviet Union.
0-394-71491-1 $7.95

Never Done: *A History of American Housework*
by Susan Strasser (1982)
The first complete history of the American housewife, American
household technology, and the ideas about housework.
0-394-70841-5 $11.95

Old Mistresses: *Women, Art and Ideology*
by Rozsika Parker and Griselda Pollock
"An important, intelligent, and provocative study of women's
position in the history of art . . . a major achievement."
—Linda Nochlin
0-394-70814-8 $10.95

The Sociology of Housework
by Ann Oakley (1975)
Oakley challenges the conventional trivialization of housework.
0-394-73088-7 $3.95

Strong-Minded Women and Other Lost Voices
of Nineteenth-Century England
by Janet Horowitz Murray
A stunning collective portrait of women's lives in
nineteenth-century England.
0-394-71044-4 $11.95

Subject Women
by Ann Oakley (1981)
A richly documented assessment of where women stand today—
economically, politically, socially, emotionally.
0-394-74904-9 $7.95

We Were There:
The Story of Working Women in America
by Barbara Wertheimer (1977)
A narrative history of women's work from pre-colonial times to the present.
"The best single volume of the history of American working-class women."
—Herbert Gutman
0-394-73257-x $7.95

Women's Work, Women's Health:
Myths and Realities
by Jeanne M. Stellman (1978)
Lays to rest several historical myths about women's working and
childbearing years.
0-394-73452-1 $5.95

Working It Out:
23 Women Writers, Artists, Scientists and Scholars
Talk About Their Lives and Work
edited by Sara Ruddick and Pamela Daniels (1977)
Candid assessments of the rewards and dilemmas of creative work.
0-394-73452-1 $6.95